GRANDMA,
Tell Me a Story

Children's devotional
stories from the farm

Cheryl L. Howard

Cheryl Lynne Howard

Illustrated by
B. Regan Greenwood

Grandma, Tell Me a Story

Copyright © 2014 by Cheryl Howard

All rights reserved. Neither this publication nor any part of this publication may be reproduced or transmitted in any form or by any means, electronic or mechanical, including photocopying, recording or any information storage and retrieval system, without permission in writing from the author or illustrator.

Unless otherwise indicated, scripture quotations are from The Holy Bible, English Standard Version® (ESV®), copyright © 2001 by Crossway, a publishing ministry of Good News Publishers. Used by permission. All rights reserved. Scripture quotations marked (NASB) taken from the New American Standard Bible®, Copyright © 1960, 1962, 1963, 1968, 1971, 1972, 1973,1975, 1977, 1995 by The Lockman Foundation. Used by permission.

978-1-4866-0530-9

Word Alive Press
131 Cordite Road, Winnipeg, MB R3W 1S1
www.wordalivepress.ca

WORD ALIVE PRESS

Cataloguing in Publication information may be obtained from Library and Archives Canada.

This book belongs to

_____

Dedication

I dedicate this book to my wonderful grandchildren, who all started reading at an early age, love the outdoors and farm life, and love to do family devotions: Ty, Clay, Anika, Owen, Maysa, and Coralie.

Introduction

Children need spiritual foundations in God if they are to become "oaks of righteousness, the planting of the Lord, that he may be glorified" (Isaiah 61:3). My husband Tom and I made family devotion time a priority to help our four children grow up in the fear and admonition of the Lord. Reading the Bible, faith stories, and devotionals around the table and before bedtime are our favorite memories with our children. Talking to them about God and praying together were everyday occurrences.

Use these true stories to build biblical truths into your children's lives, to open discussion about God, and to help answer their important questions. You will grow closer to your children and be an important mentor in their lives.

Table of Contents

One: Like A Duck Out Of Water ... 1

Two: Angel Surprise! ... 7

Three: Who Let the Dog Out? ... 13

Four: The First Recall ... 21

Five: Annie's Big-Time Escape! ... 27

Six: Oh No! Where's Annie? ... 33

Seven: Go Get 'Em! ... 39

Eight: Rescue Me! ... 45

Nine: Perseverance ... 49

Ten: Horses, Creatures of Habit ... 57

Eleven: Transformation of Bud ... 65

Twelve: Answer to Prayer ... 73

Thirteen: Who's There? ... 81

Fourteen: Vinny Stands Firm ... 85

Fifteen: Turtle Mania! ... 91

Sixteen: Bloopers! ... 101

Seventeen: Cougar Scare ... 109

Eighteen: Lowly Donkey ... 115

Nineteen: Challenging Charlie ... 121

Twenty: Trusting Charlie	127
Twenty-One: Wipeout!	133
Twenty-Two: Pure Joy	141
Twenty-Three: Teamwork	147
Twenty-Four: God's Grace	151
Twenty-Five: Visitor	157
Twenty-Six: Pet Goats	163
Twenty-Seven: Cariboo Winter	169
About the Author	177

Devotional One:
Like a Duck Out of Water

IT WAS SAD WHEN I DISCOVERED THAT A PREDATOR BIRD OR MINK HAD killed our four Indian Runner ducks. Now our pond was empty. There was no splashing or antics seen in the pond.

I decided to buy some Muscovy ducks from a farm where we routinely bought our goat milk and eggs. At that farm, the ducks didn't have a pond. Instead they just wandered and pecked in the barnyard alongside chickens.

I brought the handsome ducks home for their first real swim. For some strange reason, the ducks would not go anywhere near the pond. I tried to herd and coax them near the pond so they might get the idea of going in it themselves, but they would just fly back to the chicken coop.

Each morning when I went out to do my farm chores, I noticed strange happenings. First, one of the large Muscovy ducks was sitting in a little bucket of drinking water, which was not even big enough for its oversized bottom! It was preening itself and making quite a splash. Next, I saw some of the ducks perched up high on the chicken coop fence. Sometimes they perched there all day, especially when the snow piled high around the coop. I even found a duck visiting the inside of the coop to lay its egg in a nesting box.

What was wrong with these strange ducks? Why couldn't they be ducks and frolic and splash in the big beautiful pond?

The funniest sight was when the ducks finally made it to the pond's edge, but only stood gazing at it, refusing to go in. They were truly behaving like chickens.

The ducks came to their senses one day when they heard the beating of wings followed by a commotion in the pond. They all waddled to the pond to witness wild ducks scoot across the pond in serene fashion and duck their heads under the water for a bath. It was a fine demonstration of what real ducks do. Immediately our ducks waddled down the grassy slope and plunged into the pond with a great flurry!

They finally understood what to do and who they were. They forever abandoned their old cooped-up life of loafing around to enjoy their true identity of frolic and fun. However, I do still find the ducks stealing chicken food and laying eggs in the nesting boxes... once in a while.

Who are you? Are you like the ducks who wouldn't swim in the big pond, but preferred to settle for life in the little bucket? What are you waiting for? Listen to who God says you really are. Enjoy your life in Christ as a child of God who is a new creation.

> Therefore if anyone [child] is in Christ, he is a new creature; the old things passed away; behold, new things have come.
>
> (2 Corinthians 5:17, NASB)

Devotional Two:
Angel Surprise!

GRANDPA CAME HOME LATE ONE NIGHT AND HE WAS THE bearer of bad news. Angel, our beloved farm cat of some seven years, had been found very dead on the road right in front of our gate to the yard. Her body was quite squished.

I remember standing in the kitchen feeling shocked and not wanting the story to be true, because she was such a big part of our family. We always expected Angel to be around. She rarely was gone for more than a day. Angel was very wary of the cars and not a risk-taker. She loved to travel down the side road for visits into the bushes and across the busy main road, but she always returned.

Now, our little Angel was no more. Grandpa took her body and put it into a bag. The next day, he disposed of her body. What a sad ending for such an angelic cat.

For two days, I walked around in a fog, thinking about Angel and all her special traits that had impressed our family. She had her favourite sitting places, such as on the stairs in the sunlight, by the woodstove with the dogs, on the back of the sofa when company came, and on the rocking chair when there was a huge pile of laundry on it.

She especially loved to lie on my daughter's bed during her daytime naps. Sometimes she would even sleep way up on the carpets that were stored way up high in the rafters.

We would miss her little antics, such as swiping our legs as we went by on the stairs, or grabbing us as we sat on the sofa near her. She could purr like a motor when snoozing on your lap, meow sweetly when wanting in at the glass door from the veranda, or stand patiently while waiting to be fed morning, noon, and night.

If she was really hungry, and we forgot to feed her, she would use her paw to pry the pantry door open to get to her food dish. She was especially good at bossing every dog into its place, including the neighbourhood dogs who tried to chase her. We often found her prowling around the attic, inside the storage spaces, and sometimes we closed the door on her, forgetting her whereabouts.

By the second day of mourning, we were still feeling rather sad. That's when something amazing happened. I remember everything so clearly. I was in the kitchen with my back to the door and I sensed a fleeting movement behind me. When I turned, I was shocked to see Angel.

"Angel! You're alive!" I called in amazement.

In only a few seconds, I scooped her up into my arms and realized that the cat Grandpa had seen dead was someone else's cat that only looked like Angel, but wasn't her. Needless to say, we celebrated Angel's return to life at the Howard Farm by doting on her for quite some time.

No one likes to think about death, but in John 11:25 Jesus said, "I am the resurrection." If you are in Christ Jesus, you will be resurrected in body up into the clouds and live with Jesus forever. Jesus says to look forward to His coming. Christians don't need to fear death because Jesus has given us the victory over death. Hallelujah!

Devotional Three:
Who Let the Dog Out?

ONE DAY, A TINY PUPPY ARRIVED AT OUR HOUSE. WE ORDERED her online and she came by airplane from the Kootenay region of British Columbia. We named her Kootenay River Annie. Her breed was English Pointer. She was white with dozens of black speckles or spots all over her body. I had this dream of having a dog that would go hunting in the woods with my son Andrew and join me in all my outdoor adventures. My Granddad had a famous hunting dog named Sport who was an obedience champion. I sure loved that breed of dog and felt that Annie would be very similar. Wrong!

At first, Annie was the perfect puppy and easily passed her doggie kindergarten classes. The next set of classes was very different! On the last day of class, graduation day, Annie finally figured out who she was—a hunting dog. She took off from the arena into the woods and disappeared for a long time. Eventually she returned to the class for a drink of water, so we snagged her and promptly put her leash on. I humbly apologized for her very unexpected behaviour.

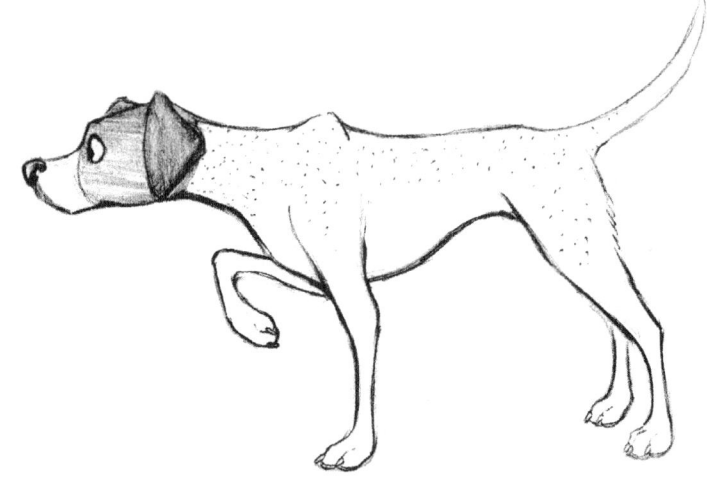

From that day forward, Annie was a hunting dog who wanted her freedom to roust out every bird within a two-mile radius of our country home. Annie managed to escape from her dog run many times when one of the farm gates was left open by accident. She would zip through any small opening to find her love of freedom in the wide open spaces of all the neighbours' farms and wood lots. Her sleek and muscular body quivered whenever she waited for her moment of escape.

Annie caused much turmoil and stress in our lives. She would often go missing for several hours, and even into the night. When we finally gave up checking at the door for her, we went to sleep. In the morning, we would find her lying on her bed on the porch after a crazy night of hunting. Some of those nights were wet and cold. She was a very determined dog!

One very frustrating character trait of Annie's was that when she had her freedom, she was elusive, or hard to catch. You had to be very clever to trick her into jumping in the car, or wait until she was exhausted and thirsty to snag her by the drinking bucket or pond. Annie had no intention of being caught until she had used up every ounce of energy and sniffing instinct.

Annie had some other very interesting habits. She would go out the front door into the flower garden in the most low and slow motion position you could imagine. Her body would freeze while her senses locked on the nearest buzzing or chirping sound in the bushes or trees. She raced after her prey when she located its whereabouts.

Sometimes Annie moved so fast that we called her a streak of white lightning. She created a deeply rutted path in the garden during her routine search of birds, bees, and any creatures that moved. Her favourite past time was snapping at bees in the air and grinding them between her teeth. She rarely got stung because of her speed. We had to electrify the bottom of the fence to keep her from digging out, and all other areas where she could jump through a tiny opening. Annie was fast, agile, and powerful. When taking her for walks on the leash, you had to wrap the leash around your body.

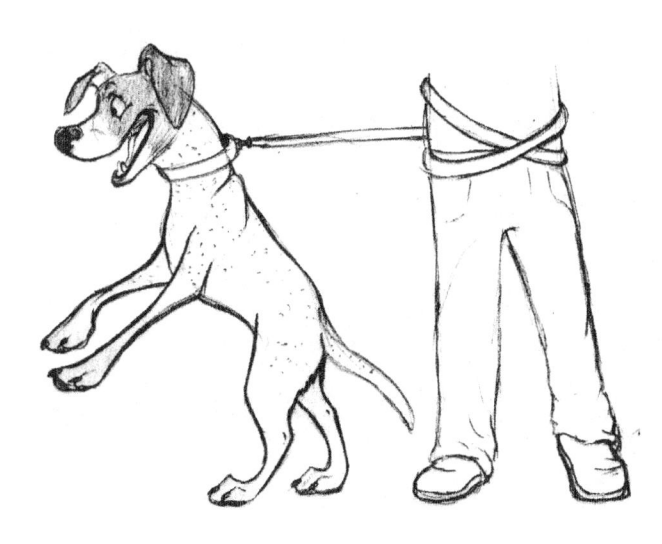

Annie loved to speak. She'd get jealous when I was on the phone and wouldn't be quiet until I was off the phone or gave her attention. If we had company over and they sat in her spot on the couch, she would stand and stare at the spot until they became unglued and moved over. She could fit in any tight spot just to make her point. Annie was so jealous of our other dog, Lady, that she twice had a big fight with her, trying to establish dominance. Lady won, of course, just by her size and volume.

Something I really liked about Annie is that she was a cuddler when indoors. Her favourite trick was to do a sneak attack in the early morning, when she could go out of bounds and leap onto our bed. Once on the bed, she would begin all kinds of antics, rolling, wiggling, cuddling, and anything to just get a few minutes of bed time. After her tossing and turning and messing up the bed covers, she would lay perfectly still, all stretched out, and wait for a very certain sound. When she heard the sound of heavy footsteps, she instantly knew the boss was coming and it was time to go! She would dash out of the bedroom to hide. It was a game she loved to play, and I must say I thoroughly enjoyed it.

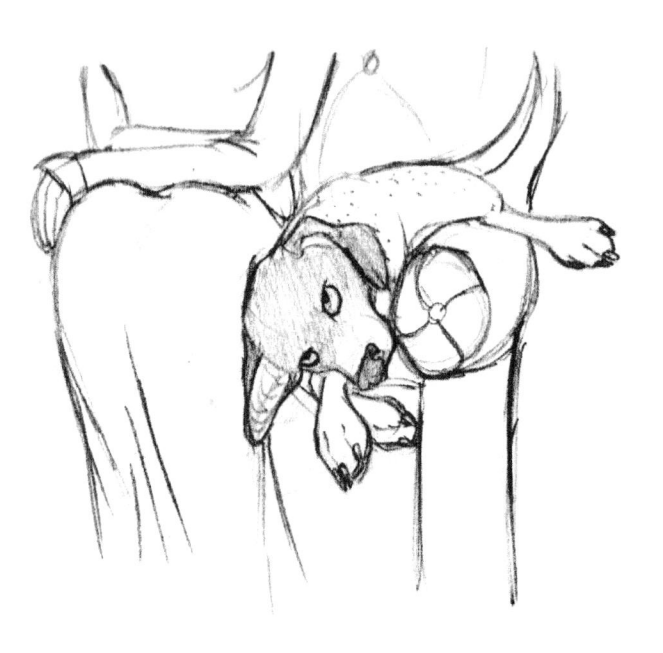

People saw Annie as a very strange dog who would never come to our call when outside. Her hunting focus and freedom was number one, and you were number two. Every time Annie escaped, we prayed for her safety from the wild animals and from the traffic on our busy road. Annie always came home. She is now eleven years old and has lived many lives that we will never know.

What can we learn from a dog like Annie? Is she all wrong, or is there something good about her existence? The Bible is very clear that our focus in life must be on Jesus. Jesus is many things to us, but most of all He is love. His love is the most precious and life-changing thing we can focus on to keep our lives healthy and happy. I'm sure the saying "he has a dogged determination" comes from a dog like Annie. Annie wasn't easily taken from her focus. Jesus had great determination during his life on earth to please the Father and stay on course, until he cried, "It is finished!" on the cross. Annie was created to hunt, and that she did well.

You were created to receive God's love and to give God's love. Learn from Annie and stay focused on God's love for you.

My eyes are ever toward the Lord, for he will pluck my feet out of the net.

(Psalm 25:15)

Devotional Four:
The First Recall

MY FRIEND WAS VISITING ME FOR A FEW DAYS AND SHE mentioned taking our dogs out for a short walk. At that time, we were looking after our son's dog, Timber, an Alaskan Malamute/Border Collie cross. So that meant taking three dogs for a walk. My friend took Lady, the more overweight and slow-paced dog named, and I took Annie, the rambunctious dog, and Timber, the oversized one, each on an arm. Off we went for a casual stroll down the quiet countryside road.

All was going very well, as the dogs went along at our pace. About halfway down the road, there was a bark in the distance, meaning a strange dog was nearby. We were quick to bring the dogs in close to check out the situation, but the strange dog continued to come very close to the road, threatening us. Timber growled and lunged forward. I was shocked at this new aggressive behaviour from Timber and quickly pulled him back to change direction. Usually, he was friendly with dogs and wanted to play. This time, he was territorial and protective. I struggled to hold Timber and Annie at the same time. Timber pulled hard two more times. He spun me around while lunging toward the large German shepherd.

On the final jerk, I got caught in the leash. It tipped me backwards, knocking me right off my feet. I fought to hold onto Annie and keep my balance. Bam! I hit the ground with my hip and shoulder. Without warning, my head smashed onto the road, sending shockwaves through my body.

During the fall, I lost grip of Annie's leash. My friend immediately came to my rescue by grabbing Timber and unwinding the leash from my body. Even though my head hurt lots, I stood up just in time to see Annie take off under the fence and into the woods. Annie's escape was dangerous for her because she was dragging a long leash that would eventually get snagged somewhere in the miles of forest, and there'd be no one to rescue her. Annie would take any opportunity to escape. Once loose, she was a streak of lightning. Freedom was her prize and she didn't surrender until she was good and tired.

In great hopelessness, I called, "Annie!" Instantly, she did a little U-turn and came back under the fence and walked through the ditch towards me. In a few seconds, she had answered my faint call and returned. I was so stunned. I reached over and picked up her leash. What a marvel that Annie had come back! My head was oh so sore. If she hadn't come back, I would have had to chase her, and that would have been the worst thing for my head, especially if I had a concussion. How thankful I was to God for turning the event around from what could have been a disaster.

Why did Annie come to me? I believe it was the Lord. God knew I shouldn't run with my injury. He was protecting me and Annie at the same time. This act of mercy was a sign of God's supernatural ways. Annie had never re-called, or come when called, since she was a puppy. It was truly God's blessing for me that day.

Since then, Annie has never re-called again, so I know it was God's work. If God can make a donkey talk to Balaam, then certainly He can make Annie re-call. The Bible says we have guardian angels, so my angel must have brought Annie back on the leash. We can't see everything God does, but we do know that He is constantly at work in our lives.

> The angel of the Lord encamps
> around those who fear him, and delivers them.
>
> (Psalm 34:7)

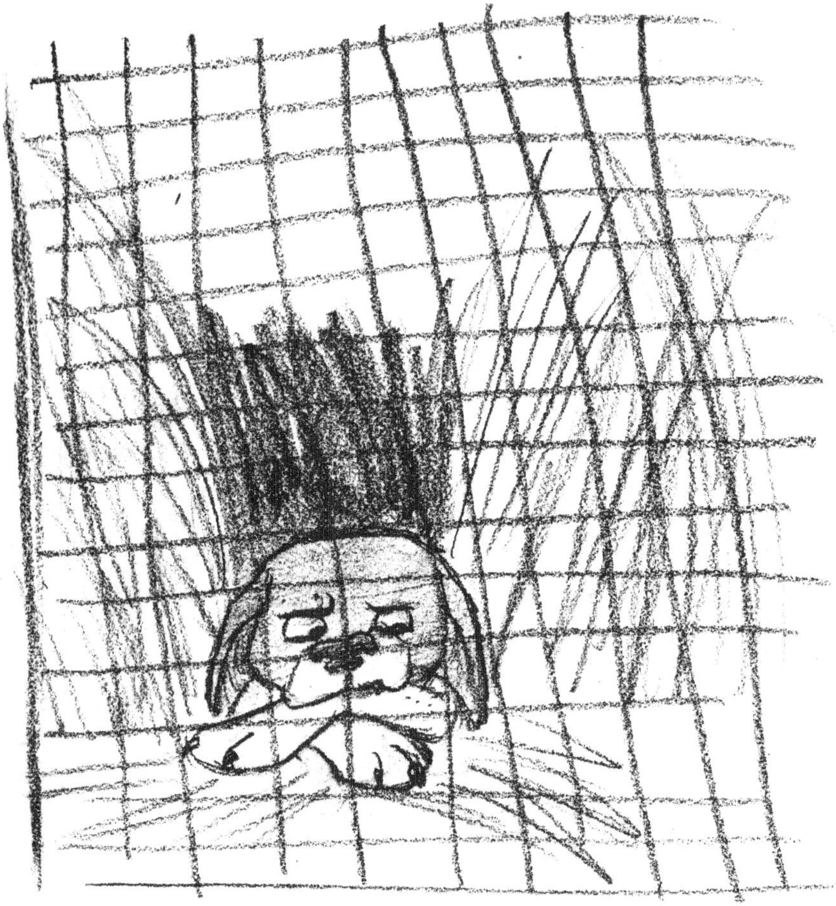

Devotional Five:
Annie's Big-Time Escape!

ANNIE HAD BEEN WITH US FOR SEVEN YEARS AT OUR HOBBY farm in the Comox Valley. Soon after her arrival, we decided to make a big move to the rich ranch land of the Cariboo region in British Columbia. When we arrived at our new farm in the summer, we knew Annie might not adjust to this big change.

Our new home had many predators that loved to eat smaller animals, especially in the winter. Annie was promptly put in a chicken run that had four-foot-high grass and a mesh fence that she could not jump. She didn't like her new pen, so Lady went in with her for company.

In no time, Annie found a soft place to tunnel under two fences for her escape. All the vast forest and fields around Annie were unfamiliar and a threat to her. Thankfully, she returned home for a much-needed drink and food. This escapade recurred several times, even after much effort was given to filling in the holes with heavy lumber and rocks.

Her determination to escape forced me to make a new plan. My neighbour, Henry, advised that if I just let her go, she would learn to come home and adjust to her surroundings. I realized that she might not survive, but because she was so determined I decided to follow his advice.

That was our plan and Annie loved it. She always had this huge grin on her face when running, and the more we called her, the faster she ran. After a week or more, she realized no one was trying to catch her, so she settled down and spent much of her time lazing in the sun around the house. Needless to say, I did have to increase her food to four meals a day to keep some weight on her very thin body.

Annie proved to be a very smart dog and survived all odds in being attacked by some prowling predators, such as a pack of coyotes that lived very close to our home. One day, Annie didn't prove to be so smart, or should I say, I wasn't so careful. Often when I drove down our long driveway, Annie would hitch a ride by jumping into the back seat when I stopped to invite her along. She was always looking for the next adventure.

This time, I was going to Forest Grove to get my goat milk and cheese. Right after I parked the car in front of the building, Annie jumped out of my open window. What a shock! She was gone in a flash and never looked back. I ran out onto the road and saw her white sleek body bounding across an open field. She was in doggy heaven!

I wondered what trouble lay ahead of her. She moved so fast from field to forest that I lost track of her. I got in the car and drove down the road. She suddenly appeared in front of the car and raced along a wide bumpy forest path. Soon, I was driving bumpity- bump along the same path. It seemed that the more I followed Annie, the more she saw it as a game of follow-the-leader.

She loved my company too much, so I stopped, turned around, and headed back to the road. My plan was to alert a few neighbours of Annie's escape and give them my phone number. Annie was heading in the direction of our home, about eight miles away. I drove home feeling rather sad not knowing if Annie would ever return. I prayed and asked God for help.

While driving home, I had a sense of peace about Annie's disappearance. I was not going to worry. About twenty minutes after arriving home, the phone rang. An older couple who lived on a field in a small mobile home had seen Annie running up and down the road. They said that she was looking for me and my car. She saw the couple and came right up to them. They promptly put a leash on her and called me. When I arrived, she was really happy to see me. It was a great reunion, and praise

God for keeping Annie safe and bringing her to this couple.

Annie taught me something valuable that day. Even though she loved her freedom, she was bonded to me and loved me more! We all love the word "freedom." The world thinks freedom is doing what we want and when we want, without any boundaries or authority correcting or disciplining us. This is a selfish and dangerous type of freedom, like Annie running wild. When you trust in God's word, receive by faith the good news of Jesus Christ's love for you, and give your heart to Jesus, only then are you truly free. You are free from eternal punishment, fear, rejection, and the power of sin and death. You will live forever with Jesus in His wonderful presence of love, joy, and peace. Freedom in Christ Jesus is the best freedom to have! Make Jesus your best friend and bond to Him.

> Live as people who are free,
> not using your freedom as a cover-up for evil,
> but living as servants of God.
>
> (1 Peter 2:16)

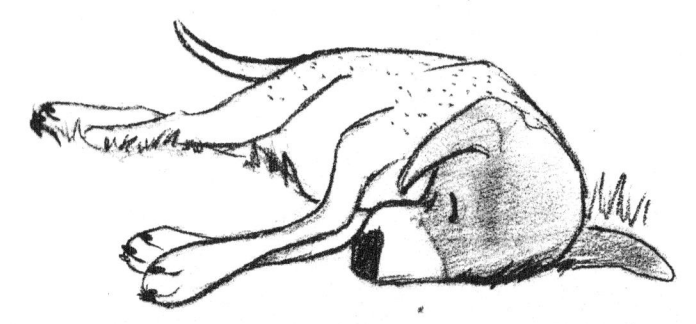

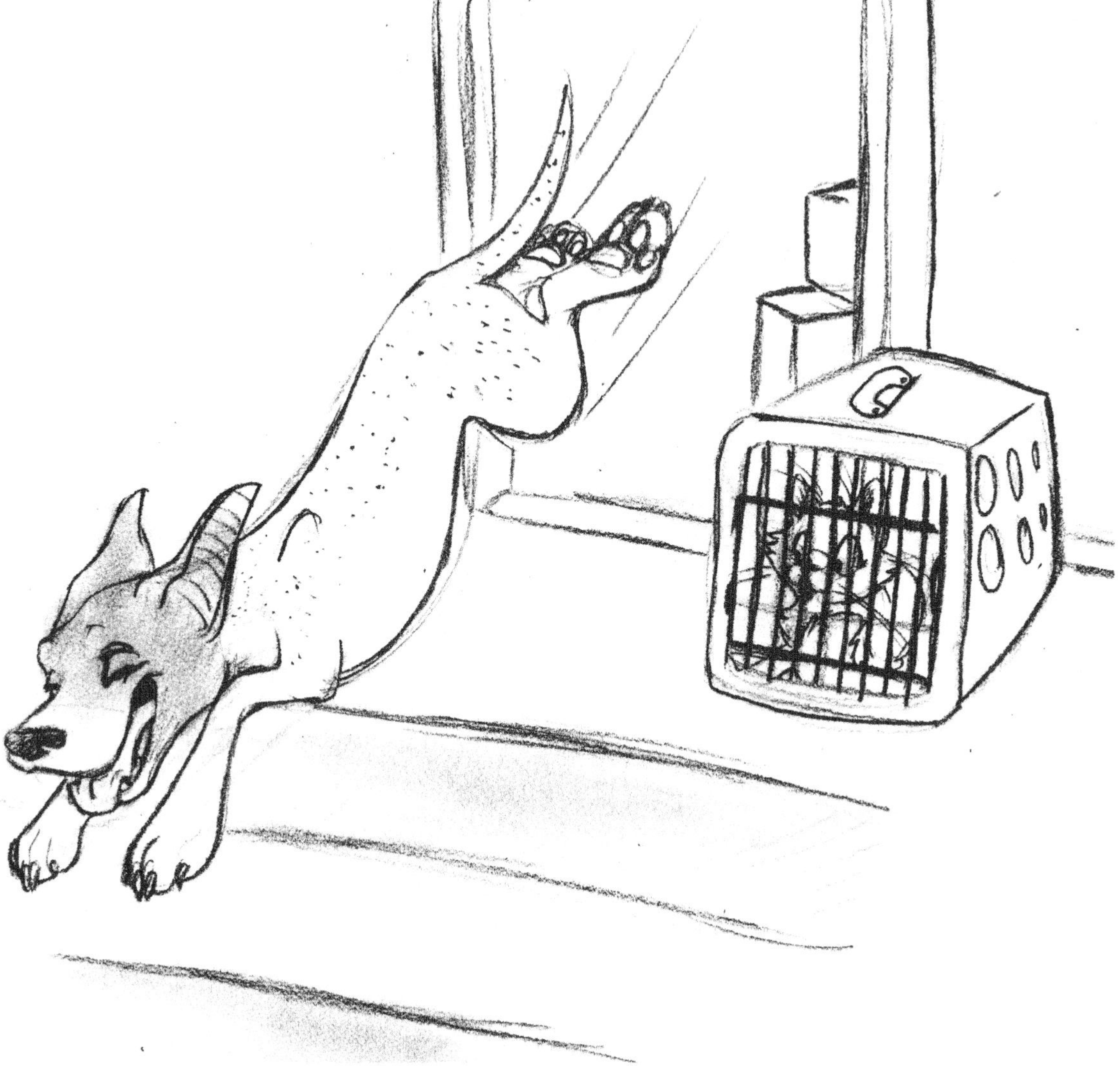

Devotional Six:
Oh No! Where's Annie?

EARLY ONE MORNING, THERE WAS BIG EXCITEMENT IN THE air! We were moving from Vancouver Island to the Cariboo for our next adventure in life. We had lots of help to move, including from our eldest daughter and grandsons who lived in China.

The moving van was getting its final load of last-minute items to be squished in somewhere. The horses were being moved up in five days and the two dogs, Lady and Annie, were coming in the car with us. Angel was already in her cage, so we didn't have to hunt for her. We had to be very organized because of a busy summer ferry. All was in place—until, that is, someone left the porch gate open. Annie zipped out and raced along the road, laughing all the way. She outsmarted us again! She was gone!

My stress level rose many notches, but I realized that only prayer would bring Annie home. We had to leave on time even if it meant leaving Annie behind. One dog was not going to upset our long-made plans. New plans would have to be made for Annie, unless of course God intervened again.

Her escape put a big blip in our plans. We were leaving in thirty minutes and Annie was nowhere to be seen or heard. She usually ran for over four hours before coming home, and on good weather days she might be gone until evening. Immediately, we put a few people into action. Our good friend and neighbour hopped into her car, with our daughter following on her bike. They raced down the road in pursuit of happy Annie.

They saw her dart in and out of driveways and disappear. The plan was to wait for her to come out and nab her. Not easy! My third daughter stopped at a place where Annie had disappeared into the bush. My friend Gail got out of her car and caught Annie's attention when she came out of a driveway. Gail patiently waited for Annie to acknowledge her and managed to draw her closer with a little enticement. She bent low to the ground and Annie was drawn to Gail's gentleness and sweetness of voice. Just when Annie got close, Gail grabbed her collar.

The game of chase finally ended and Annie was quickly transported back to our home and into the back of the car, waiting for her long trip to the Cariboo for many more adventures! God saved the day. Annie was outsmarted and caught, thanks to the work of the Holy Spirit and His angels.

Unfortunately, Annie didn't learn her lesson very well. We drove many hours to stay overnight in a small desert town called Ashcroft before arriving at our final destination. It was a very hot sunny afternoon while we sat outside on the deck overlooking the mesa trails at the back of our daughter's home. Lady and Toby (our daughter's dog) sniffed around the fenced backyard, enjoying a romp. Annie had her own ideas. She checked out the fence line and found a place to dig an exit tunnel.

I looked up and caught a glimpse of a white streak bounding across the mesa.

"Annie's out!" I exclaimed to everyone.

It wasn't an option to run after her, because the mesa was endless. She would have to learn her lesson the hard way. The mesa was covered with tiny cacti and Annie wasn't familiar with this spiny little creature that stuck like glue to the body.

The heat was unrelenting. At one point, I noticed Annie slowing down, heading in the wrong direction over the edge of the mesa toward town. I ran out, calling to her. She turned and saw me waving. At this point, her intelligence won out and she slowly jogged to the front door of the house, wanting relief from the hot sun and a much-needed drink. Needless to say, she was limping all the way.

Poor Annie. Her face, paws, and lower legs were covered with spines. It took quite some time, but eventually every tiny cactus spine was pulled out and discarded before they found their way in again. Annie was very patient with the ordeal and seemed subdued for the rest of the evening. I think she really learned her lesson.

What can you learn from this troublesome dog? Do you think she really learned her lesson about escaping? Some people would just give up on the dog and find a new home for her or have her tied up all the time. Thankfully, God isn't like that. God is very patient and gentle with us. He is long-suffering and willing to wait for us to turn back to Him. Annie should be called the prodigal dog. We rejoice every time she returns home and we give her many hugs and much praise. We do realize that one day she may not return home, and so we pray for God to watch over her daily.

Read the story of the Prodigal Son (Luke 15:11–32) to see how wonderful our heavenly Father is toward those who go their own way, ignoring the Father's love.

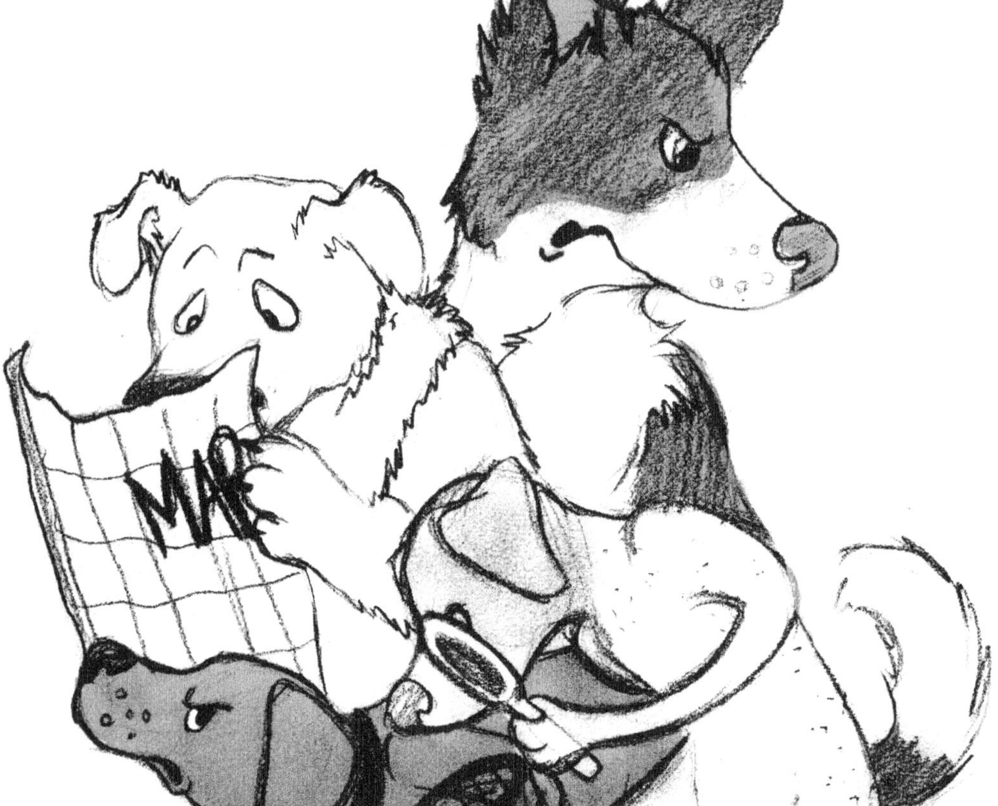

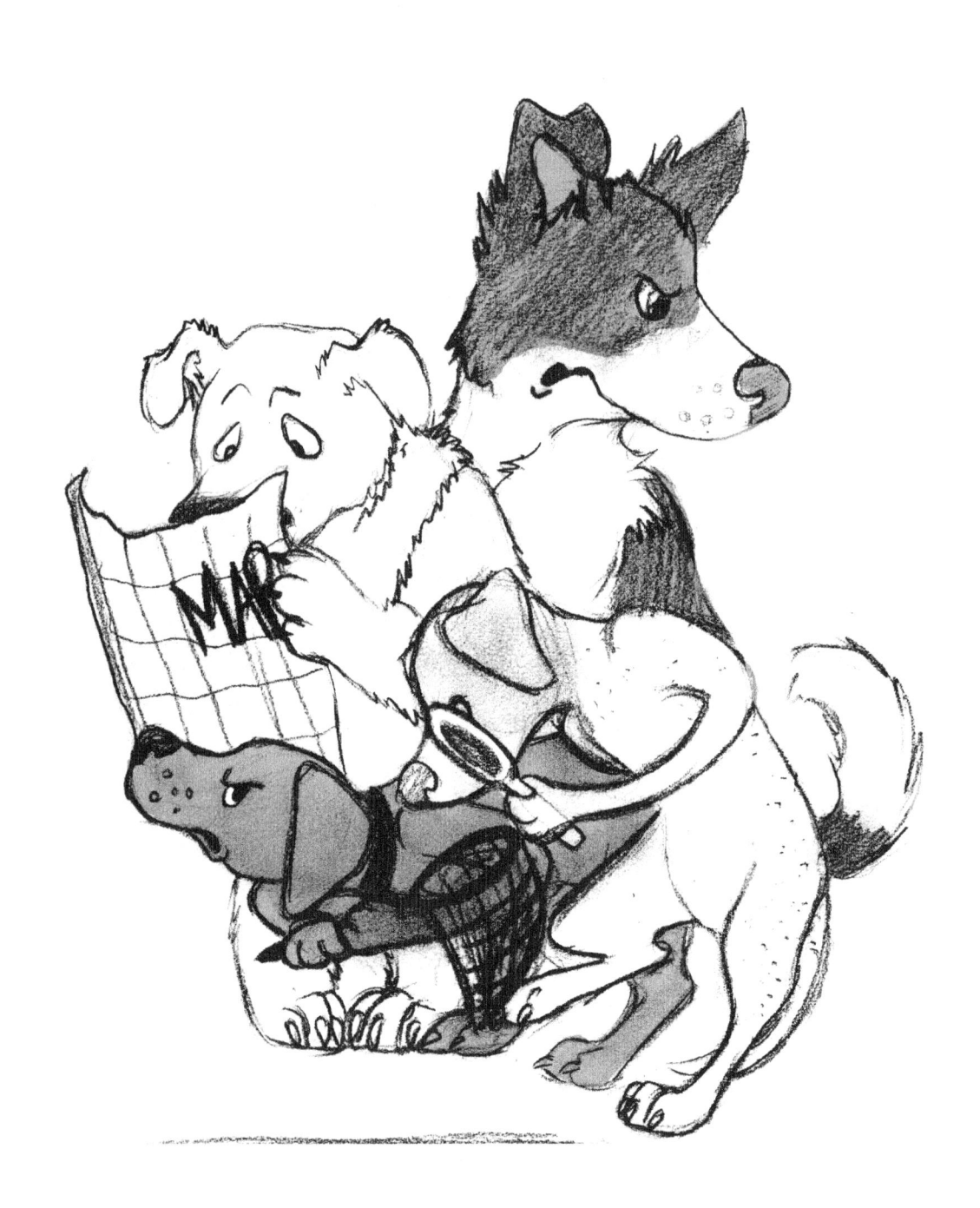

Devotional Seven:
Go Get 'Em!

HAVE YOU EVER SEEN OR HEARD OF A PACKRAT? THEY ARE fairly common in barns, abandoned buildings, and maybe in your house if they have an easy way in. When we moved to the Cariboo, I was told that we had packrats camped in our barn. I asked a neighbour, "How will I know if the packrats are still in the barn?" He answered, "You'll smell them. It's an awful smell and they're hard to get rid of. You're best to shoot them, if you can."

Even though our son had loaned us his guns for warding off predators, I was highly reluctant to shoot any critters.

Sure enough, I opened the barn door and woo-wee, what a smell! Packrats are notorious for stealing things and making quite a mess in the process. I had never seen a packrat, but I was on the lookout for one. Our four dogs were on the trail and frantic to catch a packrat, too. They disassembled the entire lumber pile many times over. Rocky, my big black horse, even got into the game of rolling boards off the pile. It was so hilarious to watch the dogs day after day being outsmarted. The rats moved from the lumber pile to the barn, to the bay garage, and back to the lumber pile.

Then came the day when the packrat made a mistake and hid behind the barn door that was latched open at all times. The dogs were frantic to reach it, but to no avail. I came along with a stick, opened the door, and prodded the packrat from its clinging position between the door and the barn wall, hoping it would fall into the dogs' jaws. No way. That packrat ran right up the wall and into the hay loft. Toby, our chocolate lab, ran to the top of the barn and into the hay loft, going crazy after the critter. Hay bales went flying down to the ground in the process. The packrat won that battle!

During the winter, the packrats seemed to burrow and hibernate underneath the lumber pile, so the dogs gave them a much-needed rest. When the spring snow melted, the dogs gave up their favourite spot by the woodstove to pursue the nasty critters again. Timber, an Alaskan Malamute, gnawed holes in the horse stall wall and Lady relentlessly scratched holes in the barn floor. Something was also hiding under the farm pickup truck, where

Timber sat waiting for hours. I knew the packrats were in trouble with four dogs on their trail. I was secretly hoping that the dogs wouldn't catch them. Packrats are real cute. They're kind of like squirrels with short ears, long tails, and soft eyes. I didn't really want them to die.

Not long into spring, Timber whined and barked at the barn door again. He had spotted something. I peeked where he was looking and, sure enough, there was a pack rat clinging in the corner behind the door. Its little beady eyes were peering at me.

I opened the door and immediately the packrat dropped to the ground where Timber waited. A second one fell closer to me. In an instant, Timber picked up the packrat and crushed it just as it gave a high-pitched screech. The other packrat began running away, so I used the manure fork in my hand to trap it and scoop it towards Timber. He was confused between the two packrats and let go of the first one to grab the second. The second one got away in the nick of time and the other one died on the spot. I noticed a pile of hay behind the door that the packrats had gathered to make a nest.

Think of the pack rat as sin—something smelly, offensive, and destructive. We often get used to sin and become friends with it, ignoring its dangers and the fact that it will cause much damage in our lives if we don't eradicate it all. One packrat remains and babies will follow. Sure enough, the next year the dogs captured and killed six more. They each were trapped in exactly the same way, behind the barn door. They weren't very smart, each falling prey to its fate.

A little sin will grow into bigger sin if you don't get rid of it all. Don't make friends with your sin. Repent of whatever is causing trouble in your life and be free of it! God loves you, but He doesn't love the sin in your life. He wants you to live free from sin and enjoy the abundant life He offers you. Be obedient to God's word and trust only in His ways.

> Let not sin therefore reign in your mortal body, to make you obey its passions.
>
> (Romans 6:12)

> For the wages of sin is death, but the free gift of God is eternal life in Christ Jesus our Lord.
>
> (Romans 6:23)

Devotional Eight:
Rescue Me!

OUR CAT ANGEL WAS HIDING UNDER THE LILAC BUSH. "SHE has a bird in her mouth," said my husband while he was hanging up a gigantic hammock between the aspen trees. I turned and saw Timber snooping under the bush after the kitty. In one quick stride, I picked up Angel and saw that the tiny bird was alive. Angel allowed me to gently pry the baby bird from her mouth. Both Timber and Angel wanted that bird, but I had rescued it from the jaws of death and there was no giving in! The brown- and black-striped tiny bird fit nicely into my palm with my other hand. Its beady eyes were dark and active. My quiet hands could feel its heart pumping so hard that I knew it was in shock.

I thought, *Oh, please don't die, little bird. You are so special and must live, for your mother is somewhere looking for you. Now where did you come from, little one?*

I turned and looked up at all the trees and bird boxes. Movement caught my eye and, yes, there was a bird flying overhead by a bird box. Suddenly it flew into the bird house and peered out at us as if to say, "That's my baby you have." My husband promptly got a tall ladder to return the baby bird to its nest.

I readied myself to climb the ladder with one hand and the baby bird in the other. The mother bird had flown away, so it was perfect timing. Just when I had reached the top of the ladder, the baby bird tried to flutter off. I held it firmly and managed to squeeze it like toothpaste into the small opening. Thankfully, the baby bird landed safely in the nest and didn't try to leave. We watched the bird house for a while from the ground, but no eyes peered out. I prayed that the mother would continue to care for her baby and it would see happy days ahead, especially killing the many mosquitoes that taunted us daily.

Have you ever rescued something or someone from disaster? It's a great feeling to do a kind deed. There's a verse in the Bible that says how much God cares for the little sparrow and how much more He cares for us, so we don't need to worry about our basic needs in life. We are more precious to God than a little sparrow. Not one is lost without Him knowing, so we can trust in God's care for us.

Can you see yourself safely in His palm? When we invite Jesus to come into our hearts and be our Lord and Saviour, God rescues us from the kingdom of darkness and puts us into His kingdom of light and love. God is kind and good to all His children. You are safe in Him.

> Therefore I tell you, do not be anxious about your life, what you will eat or what you will drink, nor about your body, what you will put on. Is not life more than food, and the body more than clothing? Look at the birds of the air: they neither sow nor reap nor gather into barns, and yet your heavenly Father feeds them. Are you not of more value than they?
>
> (Matthew 6:25-26)

Devotional Nine:
Perseverance

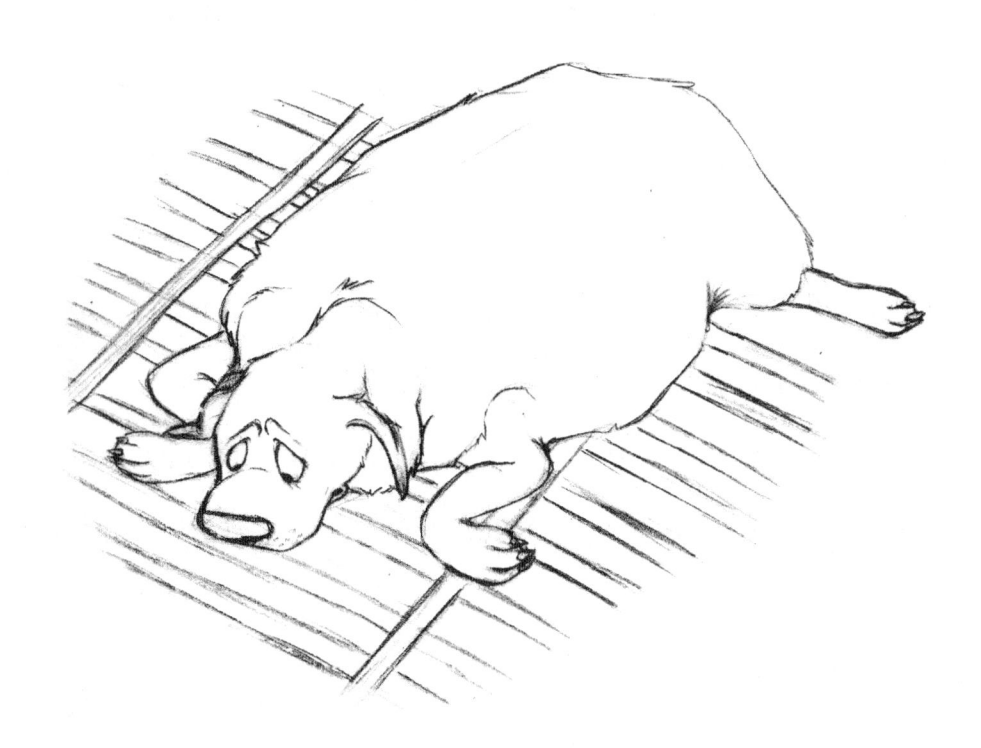

DO YOU KNOW WHAT THE WORD "PERSEVERANCE" MEANS? Sometimes the best way to describe a word is to create a word picture. Our dog, Lady, is my best word picture for perseverance. We adopted her at an animal shelter for homeless pets. She came to us very overweight. We tried to fix her problem by diet and exercise, but there was no change. I thought she lost weight at one point, but everyone in the family said, "No, you're just imagining it. She looks the same as always." When it came time to move to the Cariboo, Lady was so out of shape that she could barely climb stairs or walk a quarter-mile down the road without huffing and puffing and sitting in the middle of the road for a rest.

After moving to the Cariboo, I got really serious about monitoring Lady's exercise, because she was a fantastic guard dog and loyal friend. I thought she might have a heart attack or seizure if we didn't do something drastic.

Having three dogs for her to play with really helped her move about vigorously for a few minutes a day, but she truly needed some serious walking. I loved to walk along our trails and Lady was my constant companion—that is, if I walked slowly, at her pace!

I'll never forget Lady's first introduction to crossing our cattle guard at the end of the driveway. With exuberance, Lady stepped out onto the cattle guard and promptly fell through the gaping spaces. She was plum flattened with her legs through the grate. I was horrified to see her so helpless. Lady was probably 125 pounds and mostly limp weight. Fortunately, I had a leash and wrapped it around her belly and started pulling. Lady got the hint and began to struggle onto her feet and try to stand on the cattle guard. She made it. Each step forward was difficult, but she got to the other side.

From that time on, the cattle guard became a huge barrier to Lady, but she always persevered and made it to the other side. Eventually, I placed a long flat board along the edge of the cattle guard so Lady could make her way easily to the other side. Sometimes, just to show off, Lady would cross it the hard way and take off running. She was a real trooper and so much fun to have along.

One day, I decided to go exploring on some new trails, and after a fair time I got lost. The other two big dogs disappeared and our hunting dog, Annie, ran large circles around us. Lady began to tire to the point of sitting down on the trail, puffing like an engine under stress. I became her greatest cheerleader by clapping and calling, "Come on, Lady, you can do it, good girl, keep going, Lady!" She would get up and trudge on. I felt bad for her, but I didn't want to leave her alone and find my own way. Lady never gave up during the two solid hours we wandered our way out of the trails. She responded to each of my cheerleading sessions. When we arrived at our home, the other dogs greeted us with glee. They were the impatient ones who knew the way but hadn't waited for us.

Another day, I wanted to explore the forest without going on the trails. We clambered over logs and under logs of great size. Many times, Lady had no way to go but over a log and she would whine until she decided on her route. Sometimes she would get stuck hanging over a log and look absolutely ridiculous, but we came to her rescue. Wherever we went, she tried to follow.

I love to run, and there's no way I can leave the property without Lady in pursuit. She knows when she joins me that it'll be up and down hills, hot and dusty, buggy and tiresome, but she yips and yaps when I call, "Let's go for a run, Lady!" She wags her tail, waddles her hips, and starts off with a very energetic jog. At times, she'll even take off at a sprint when she hears the familiar high-pip sound of a nearby gopher.

In my routine runs, I meet Lady on the return trip. She's usually found trudging very slowly. We head back together. When we get to the hills, she lags far behind, barely moving one paw in front of the other. Once my run is complete, I double back to find Lady. What an amazing sight when I see her tail wagging, hips swinging, and two dots above her eyes sweetly saying, "I'm coming."

During the winter, we took our first walk to Lower Lake and then across the frozen waters. Lady, of course, had to come. She loved the snow, but it was very deep, so her short legs and heavy chest had to plough through a three-foot depth. Two of us went ahead to break a path, but the snow was still very difficult for Lady. She just kept putting one paw in front of the other, hoping to get there eventually.

After crossing the lake, we found a trail leading up the other side into the forest, which would join with a ski trail back to our home. The snowy trail leading up from the lake was steep without tracks to help us climb. Lady was a real trooper. She persevered, one step at a time.

After much difficulty, she got smart and found an easier way under the bushes. Sometimes she went way off-course to find that patch of thinner snow. Once on top of the hill, we had a long way to go with her body pushing snow the entire way. I constantly turned to encourage Lady. She would respond with a tail wag and pick up her pace for a few strides.

Her perseverance since coming to the Cariboo has been a huge witness to me of a dog with heart and desire to persevere, no matter the cost.

So, what does the Bible say about perseverance? In Ephesians 6:18, the Apostle Paul tells Christians to pray with perseverance, until the end, and not to grow tired, but to be alert, aware of what is going on in the spiritual world. Also, in 1 Timothy 4, the Apostle Paul encourages believers to be good servants of Christ Jesus by toiling and striving in training to live godly lives. In 1 Timothy 4:16, Paul uses the word "persist" instead of "persevere" for practicing and devoting ourselves to be trained in the words of faith and in the teachings of Jesus Christ.

We need to persist in living godly lives, because the world around us tries to teach us differently and take us in its direction. Paul compares the Christian life to athletes running a race according to the rules, running for the prize and never giving up or turning back. Our hope is the same, as we set our eyes on Jesus, the author and finisher of our faith.

> Brothers, I do not consider that I have made it my own. But one thing I do: forgetting what lies behind and straining forward to what lies ahead, I press on toward the goal for the prize of the upward call of God in Christ Jesus.
>
> (Philippians 3:13-14)

Devotional Ten:
Horses, Creatures of Habit

THIS SPRING IN THE CARIBOO WAS VERY WET. IT WAS unusual for such a semi-arid climate. Our horses did well adjusting to the cold and snowy winter, but springtime proved a little challenging for us all. Last haying season, we were haying by the first week of July. This year, we didn't get on the fields until a month later. The horses had eaten all their grass in the upper field, where we don't hay, and they had nothing left to eat for a few weeks.

Grandpa and I got into a routine of feeding the horses fresh-cut grass from the areas we don't hay, like along the driveway and fence lines. They were like clockwork waiting for their noon, afternoon, and evening hay feeds. Prince always gave a neigh when he heard the wheelbarrow come up the driveway with a stack of freshly cut grass. It was the easiest catch of a meal for them, no grazing required.

Grandpa and I have learned over the years how important it is to get the horses into a feeding routine. Horses are creatures of habit and get stressed if something out of the ordinary changes. It's best not to have too tight a schedule, so the horses learn to be flexible in feeding times. We humans are not always punctual.

It was obvious that the horses had lost weight and we needed to get them on the grass. The hayfield we normally put them on after haying was still bogged down in water from the heavy spring rains. It would be another few weeks for the haying, so we devised a plan to hay a high area that was covered in red clover and daisies, fence it off from the hayfield and then turn them out.

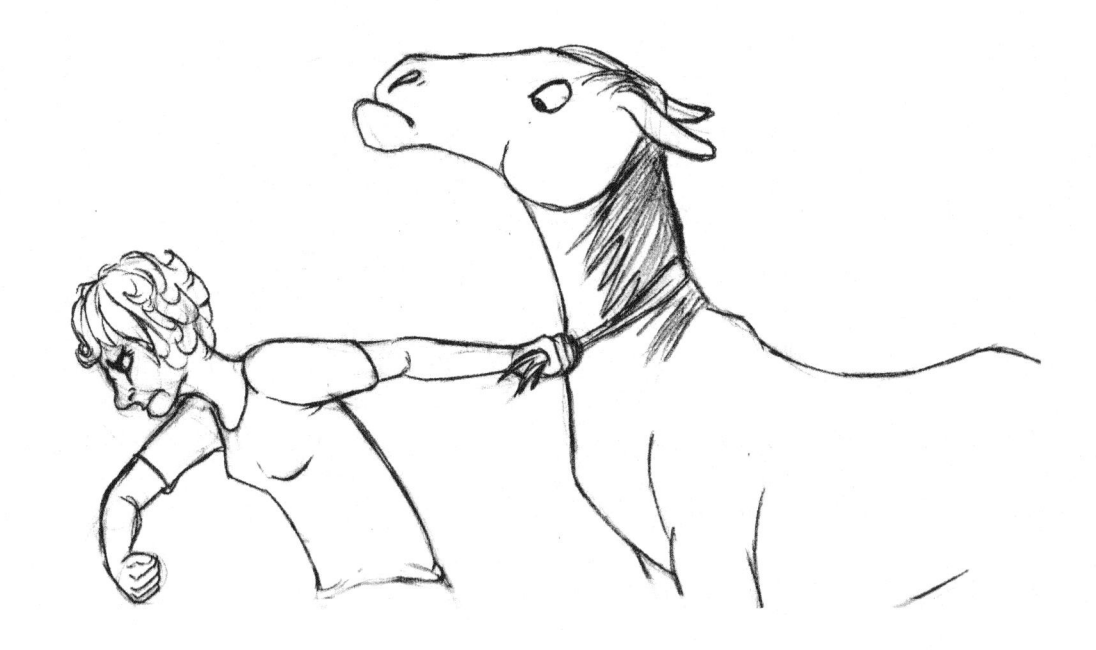

We spent a few days fencing the hayfield off, and then came the day to let the horses out on the lovely fresh grass. I was so happy for this day and I knew the horses would be, too. I called the horses up from their overgrazed pasture and they came up with curious looks on their faces. I beckoned for Rocky and Prince to follow me to the pasture. Prince couldn't be pulled along by his mane. It was their feed and siesta time up at the barn, not time to go back out on the pasture. I tried putting my shirt around

Rocky's neck to lead him out, but we both ended up in the bushes. Rocky wasn't going to miss his freshly cut grass. Little did he and the other two horses know that a whole pasture of green grass waited for them just around the corner and up the hill. They weren't up to trying something new or trusting my guidance.

I went back to the barn and got Prince's halter and lead rope. Once I put the halter on Prince, we trudged slowly back up the hill to the far pasture. Prince was so reluctant that I had to pull him the entire way. Of course, the other two horses followed, being herd animals. When we were very close to the open gate that had been closed since last year, the horses started to pick up their pace.

Once at the gate, I had to pull Prince to a stop because he finally saw his long-awaited opportunity for fresh grass. Some of the grass was eight feet tall. The horses entered the pasture very excitedly, but slowly, not sure if they were dreaming. They first went to the hay on the ground that we hadn't baled yet and thought that was good, but then realized they could have dessert, and off to the lovely sweet grass they went, settling into their old familiar munching routine.

The next morning when I put the horses out, there was no hesitation in their minds. They raced out to the back field, frolicking and enjoying the new grass on the high hill. I chuckled, thinking, *Don't get too comfortable, horses. There are more changes to come.*

We can be just like those horses, creatures of habit, wanting to stick with the same old routine. When some great opportunity or new direction is offered, we might not even recognize it, for fear of not getting what we're familiar with. The Holy Spirit is our guide, and when he taps us on the shoulder to get our attention to go in a different direction, we need to be sensitive and pay attention.

The life of a Christian is one of many adventures, involving courage and an open and willing heart. We need to remain flexible and open to change. A good student is willing to learn new things and not get stuck in the deep ruts of the boring and routine life. Routine has importance in our lives, but not so much that we don't depend on the direction and guidance of the Holy Spirit. So, be willing to try new things and adapt to your new surroundings, even if it means change. Psalm 34:8 says, "Oh, taste and see that the Lord is good!" God invites us to get to know Him. People know the world and its ways very well, but not the ways of God.

> For my thoughts are not your thoughts, neither are your ways my ways, declares the Lord. For as the heavens are higher than the earth, so are my ways higher than your ways and my thoughts than your thoughts.
>
> (Isaiah 55:8-9)

Can you think of ways that God is different than the world? What might be some of God's thoughts? If you read Philippians 4:7-8 and Colossians 3:2, you will discover God's thoughts.

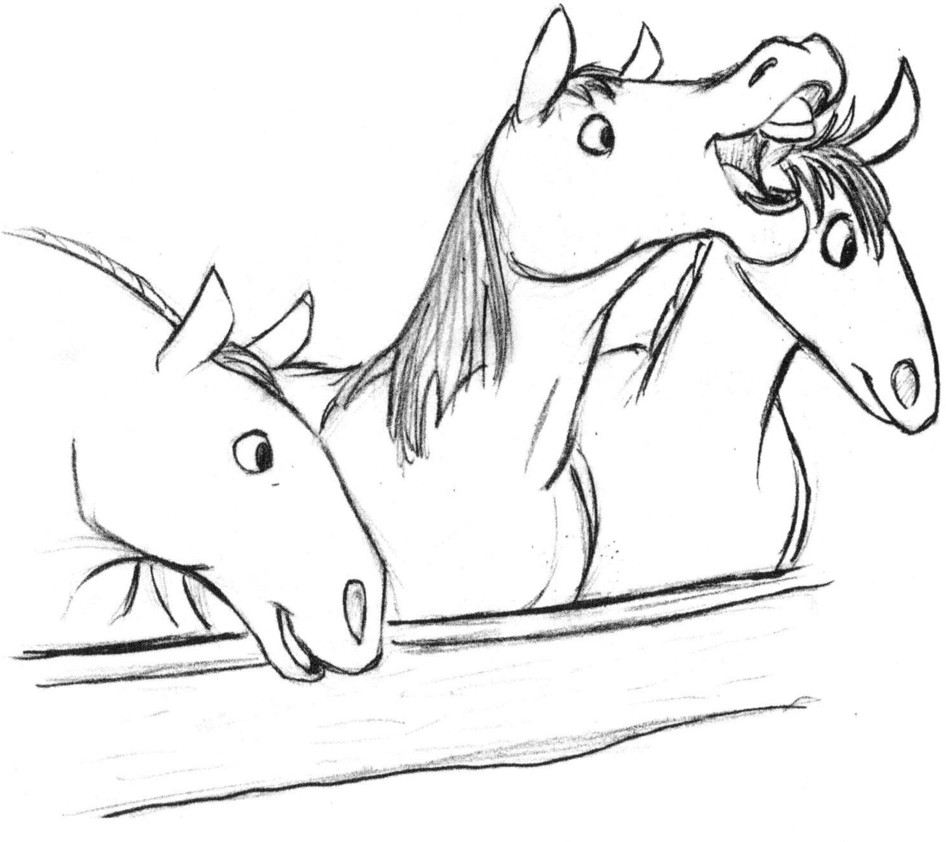

Devotional Eleven:
Transformation of Bud

AFTER LIVING FOR ELEVEN YEARS IN OUR WONDERFUL home on forty acres in the Comox Valley, we decided to move to a smaller acreage not far away. Our daughter Grace wasn't happy about the move. She didn't want change and she loved her perfect life on the hobby farm surrounded by acres of woods. I wanted everyone happy about the move, so we offered her a peace token: a kitten! Grace loved kittens and really wanted one of her own.

We had never been able to have a kitten before because of Bud. Bud was a yellow lab who had a reputation for killing cats. Five so far! He killed a cat when we went to visit a friend. The cat was in its own yard and Bud raced across the lawn to snatch the cat with a vengeance. We adopted Bud when he was mature, so we never knew why he hated cats. When our eldest daughter rescued abandoned kittens in the forest and brought them home, they lived only a short while out in the barn before Bud discovered them. Cats weren't safe around Bud.

Somehow I felt that God would show us how to help Bud change his mind about cats. When we moved, we adopted a six-week-old kitten. Grace called her Angel, but she was only an angel when she wanted something, like food.

Around the same time, we also bought another dog, Julie. She was part Jack Russell and part beagle. Julie was a pup and Angel was a kitten. Our plan was to put the two of them together to train Bud. We kept the kitten in the house and allowed Julie to romp and play with the kitten whenever Julie came indoors. They soon became great friends. Julie only knew that kittens were fun—and bossy! Bud, of course, wasn't allowed anywhere near the kitten. He would stand at the front door, peering curiously through the glass to watch the kitty and Julie chase each other and then fall asleep by the woodstove. Bud could hardly wait until that kitty was his dinner. It was written all over his chops. During winter, Bud was never allowed in the house with the kitty unless we moved her to Grace's bedroom for safety.

One day, I felt it was time to let Bud in the house with Angel, but Bud had to be on a leash. Bud would lick his chops and slobber heavily, while watching her strut around the house and play with Julie. Sometimes Bud would lunge for her, but always the leash held him fast. Angel only knew that dogs were trustworthy and fun to play with. I could see that more time was needed to train Bud not to kill cats.

Gradually, Bud no longer licked his chops when he was around the kitty. He looked as if he wanted to play, too, so I allowed him to come in the house without a leash to see if he would behave. We were all ready to pounce on Bud if he made a wrong move. If we sensed Bud moving too quickly towards Angel, we would say, "No, Bud!" And Bud would listen. After many trials of allowing Bud in the house, he began to pass the test, but we were always with him.

Angel couldn't stay in the house forever. Spring was soon upon us and it was time for her to venture outside and enjoy another part of life. So out she went and in went Bud. Bud was now on the inside looking out, and Angel was exploring her new and fascinating world of butterflies, birds, moles, and crickets. She also discovered cars, lawn mowers, horses, ducks, and chickens. Oh, she loved the outdoors! After a few weeks of exploration outdoors, it was time to let Bud out with her. If Bud respected and liked Angel, would he still kill her?

Today was test day! Out went Bud. Would Bud see her and chase her? Would Angel run away and the chase begin? Could they be friends? Bud met her outside in the garden and started to lick his chops. Angel held her ground and didn't move; after all, Bud was her friend. Bud tried to go for her, but she swatted Bud on the face. Bud backed off, quite taken aback. Bud was no longer the king pin. Angel was, and she wasn't afraid of the big bad wolf at all. She was angelic and quickly forgave Bud, thinking he had just gotten a little rambunctious. Soon Bud learned a new way of peace. He gave in to that courageous kitty who thought all dogs loved her because of her wonderful relationship with Julie.

What a sigh of relief for all of us when there were no more worries. Bud completely accepted Angel as the head of the family, and so did we. Transformation took place in Bud's mind and heart. He learned to accept something new. Bud had always reacted without thinking when he saw a cat, but now his heart told him differently. Angel and Bud became good friends, and they would spend many hours together during the winter lying in front of the woodstove, along with Julie.

Jesus said that He came to give us life abundantly. To live this abundant life, we must first receive Christ into our hearts and let His love change us. When our minds are renewed, we can behave differently and have a loving relationship with people, even people we never used to like or care for.

Jesus says that we are to be changed to become more like Him, full of love, mercy, compassion, joy, and peace. Jesus wants His love to rule in our hearts and minds, not hatred, anger, hurt, strife, jealousy, envy, or unforgiveness. Jesus wants us to live in peace with all people.

Will you let Jesus's love come into your heart and change your thinking and actions towards yourself and others? If so, you can enjoy that abundant life Jesus offers each of us.

> Do not be conformed to this world, but be transformed by the renewal of your mind, that by testing you may discern what is the will of God, what is good and acceptable and perfect.
>
> (Romans 12:2)

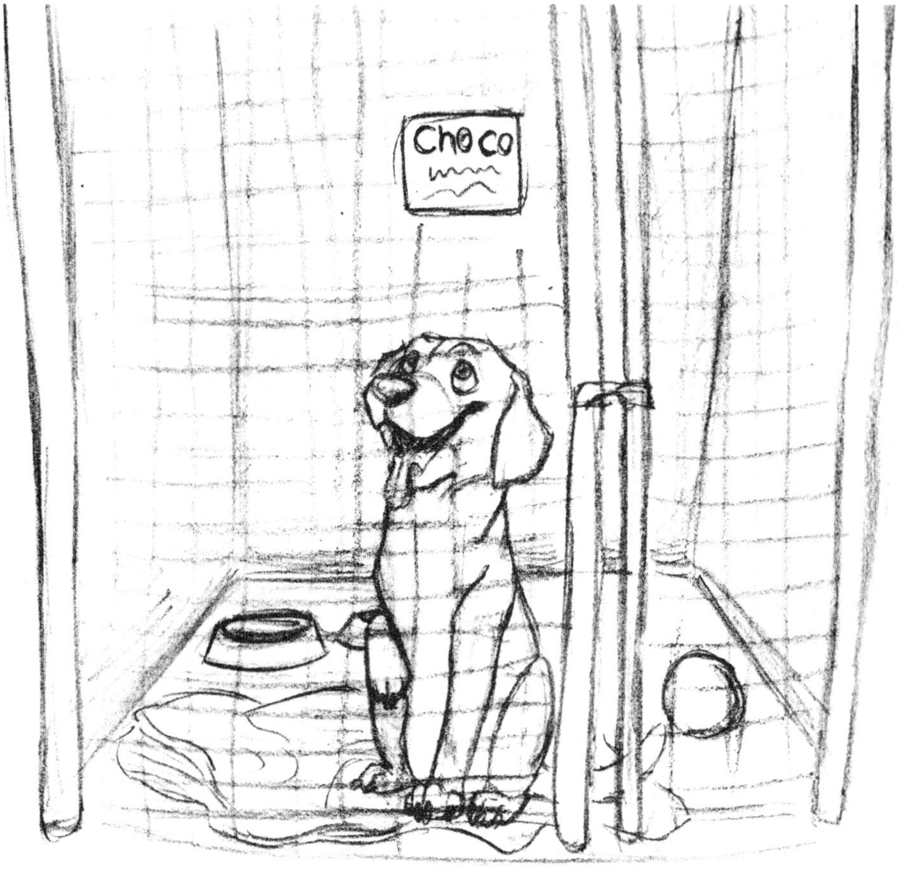
Choco

Devotional Twelve:
Answer to Prayer

WE HAD A YOUNG FAMILY OF THREE CHILDREN WHILE LIVING in a rural area of Maple Ridge. Our hobby farm was delightful with horses, goats, chickens, a dog, and a cat. It was always my dream to have a chocolate lab dog, so we were on the lookout for one. Chocolate labs are very expensive and our budget didn't fit the cost, so we periodically checked with the local humane society.

One day, we went into Richmond to visit my parents, and while there I phoned the humane society. It seemed quite amazing that they had a chocolate lab up for adoption. We quickly went in and adopted Choco, a wonderful big lab. He had dark, dreamy eyes to match his colour and he fell in love with our energetic children and hobby farm. Thank you, God, for giving us such a special surprise. It was so rare to adopt a chocolate lab, since they are a very expensive breed.

After a while, we noticed some very strong character traits in Choco. He loved to dig up old bones and relics from our yard. He always had to have a big stick in his mouth for chewing and fetching. He would hound you for hours to toss the stick so he could play the most exciting game of fetch. He'd slobber all over the stick, and you in the process. Choco was a perfect fit with our other dog, Fanny, and a companion to our children while they played outdoors.

Christmas season was upon us and I was furiously baking festive goodies. In my haste, I failed to notice that I had put the wrong ingredient in the shortbread cookies—that is, until I took a taste of the uncooked dough. Yuck! Instead of icing sugar, I had added cream of tartar, and lots of it! When baking with cream of tartar, the recipe usually only calls for one-eighth of a teaspoon. I had no choice but to throw out the cookie dough. Thinking about Choco's digging habits, I asked my husband to bury the dough really deep in the backyard. We had to go out for the afternoon, but we felt okay about the buried dough and Choco being loose in the yard. Perhaps the Holy Spirit was trying to get my attention, but I went out and dismissed any afterthoughts.

When we came home in the late afternoon, Choco wasn't looking too good. By the next day, we realized that he had, in fact, dug up the dough and eaten it. I promptly took him to the vet. Then we noticed that he wouldn't drink water or eat. The vet said he would be fine in a few days and sent us home. I remember sitting with Choco's head on my lap. He was weak and listless. His eyes were droopy and his face was sad. We prayed much for Choco, but our prayers seemed to fade into the distance. In four days, he died from the poisonous cream of tartar. How I regret having not paid closer attention to the Holy Spirit when we buried the dough. It was a lesson to be learned.

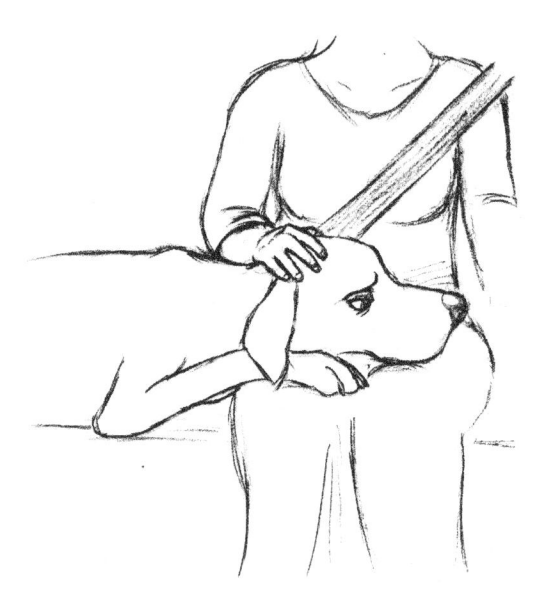

We all cried. It was a sad day to witness our beloved Choco's death. His death was like a sting to our souls. I believe the children's spirits were wounded, too. They had simply trusted God to heal Choco, and it didn't happen. What now, God? Where was Your power and compassion? Losing a pet is nothing compared to losing a family member or friend, of course. This wasn't the first pet we lost, but Choco was so dear to us.

In time, we accepted Choco's tragic death and moved on. My prayer was, "God, how will You rebuild trust in our children?" Several months later, God answered my prayer. We came home from an outing and found a chocolate lab on our upstairs balcony. We all looked intently at the dog, because he was identical to our Choco. This chocolate lab had a collar and a torn rope hanging from his neck. He looked sick, and yet so happy to see us. Of course we fed him, hugged him, and gave him a good looking over.

We found a tattoo in his ear and decided to take him to the nearby vet. The vet put his number in the system and contacted the owner. The owner had tied the lab up every day before going to work. The dog had been unhappy and broke free. He was full of parasites and not cared for very well. We so desperately wanted to adopt him, but we had to wait eleven days before adoption was possible. The previous owner didn't know if he wanted him back.

We saw that the dog was fading quickly, and we didn't want to see him die an untimely death like our Choco. We pleaded with the vet to contact the man and ask if we could adopt the dog early. Praise the Lord, the man finally gave in and said yes and released the dog to us a few days later. We immediately had him treated for parasites, fed him huge meals, and loved on him something big! We named him Choco 2, and he had exactly the same traits of log-carrying, fetching, and digging as Choco 1.

Choco 2 eventually died of old age, but he did survive a cougar attack when we moved to Vancouver Island. That was a miraculous healing, as the vet had given up on treating him. God gave us the wisdom to apply aloe poultices, which worked very quickly in getting rid of all the poison in his wounds. It is important to ask God for wisdom when praying for healing. God works healing in many different ways.

Have you ever lost a pet or loved one? Death is a natural part of life and we're usually not prepared to lose them. What we discovered as a family is that God saw our grief and had a plan to bless us and rebuild our faith in Him. There may be loss, but there is always a new beginning and a new blessing on the horizon just waiting to be discovered. Trust God even in the dark times and praise Him for His goodness.

Psalm 23 has some comforting verses for those people going through loss. God has put eternity in our hearts, and we have a living hope that when our body dies, our spirit is present with the Lord.

For I am sure that neither death nor life, nor angels nor rulers, nor things present nor things to come, nor powers, nor height nor depth, nor anything

else in all creation, will be able to separate us from the love
of God in Christ Jesus our Lord.

(Romans 8:38-39)

Jesus took the sting out of death when He died on the cross to take the punishment for our sins. There is no power in death for the believer. In John 14:1-4, Jesus says,

> Let not your hearts be troubled. Believe in God; believe also in me.
> In my Father's house are many rooms. If it were not so, would I have told you
> that I go to prepare a place for you? And if I go and prepare a place for you,
> I will come again and will take you to myself, that where I am you may be also.
> And you know the way to where I am going.

Devotional Thirteen:
Who's There?

GRANDPA CAME RUNNING INTO THE HOUSE LATE AT NIGHT, calling, "Come quickly if you want to see something interesting!" Our three children and I followed Grandpa outside. We walked into the quiet pitch-black darkness, me reaching for my son Andrew, so I wouldn't stumble.

Grandpa directed the two girls to hold his large flashlight high to illuminate the top of our flag pole near the pond. Behold, we saw a tall feathered bird perched like a statue. It didn't take long to recognize the bird as a barn owl. It stared down at us with its saucer glowing eyes and heart-shaped face. What a sight! It was so special to see an owl up close. Surprisingly, the beam of light didn't frighten it away. Periodically, its head swivelled towards different sounds. An owl was certainly a most curious and puzzling bird.

Grandpa had first spotted the owl when he went out to feed the horses. He happened to glance sideways at a looming shadow moving out of the chicken coop where numerous rats had burrowed underground. His unexpected appearance must have frightened the owl away.

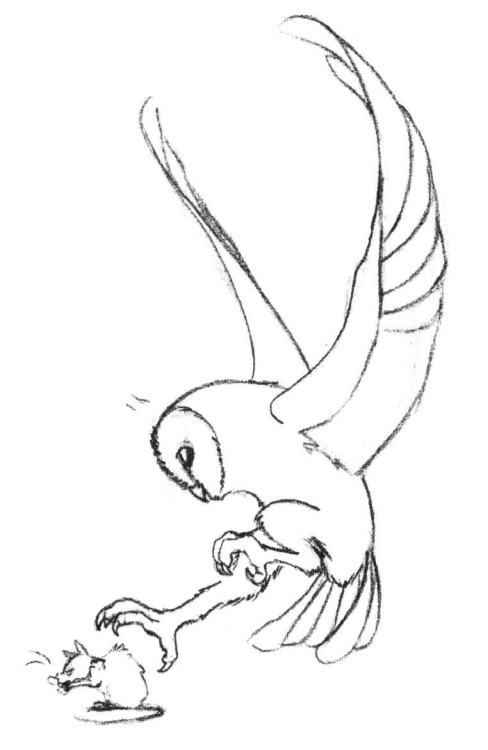

Every once and a while, a brave rat would race out from a hole and grab some grain left behind from the chickens. Not far away, the predator owl would wait for a rat to appear. The owl, a night creature, can detect the slightest movement because of his acute sense of hearing and well-developed binocular vision. In one fell swoop, the rat is clinched in its claws and whisked away for a scrumptious meal. If you look carefully on the ground, you may find the spit-out remains of an owl's prey, a lump of feathers, fur, and bones. Owls can't chew their prey, so they spit them out. Perhaps you can solve the mystery of what the owl ate for dinner.

Owls feed at night to avoid competing with other predators, such as bald eagles and hawks. They have special feathers which reduce the noise of their flapping wings to sneak up on their prey. The structure of an owl's foot allows it to grasp its prey with greater ease. Food is easily torn with its sharp and long-hooked beak, mostly hidden under a pile of feathers. Not all owls hoot, but most screech, scream, and hiss their loud and low noises into the night. God certainly had a plan in mind when He made barn owls.

I was so thankful for the owl's help in depleting our high rat population. We had so many rats that year that they could be easily seen on a hot summer's day playing near the barn door. They could also be heard scurrying under the hay bales and up the rafters when we opened the barn door. That is not cool! The owl came to our rescue and gave us a wonderful family memory!

The Creator of the universe can be known by studying His creation. Owls are odd birds which show us God's amazing wisdom and power. Take time to explore and investigate God's world of wonders. Start a nature collection of bugs, butterflies, flowers, or leaves. Try studying a landscape or creature and draw it in a sketchbook. Be a student of God's handiwork for life and watch your faith in God grow!

> The heavens declare the glory of God,
> and the sky above proclaims his handiwork.
>
> (Psalm 19:1)

Devotional Fourteen:
Vinny Stands Firm

MY HUSBAND AND I WERE OFF ON A HORSE RIDE. WE HAVE some great trails right next to our property. This ride would be different because we wanted to get across the cattle guard to explore new trails down the road. One problem was that the horses couldn't cross a cattle guard because it was made of steel rails that crisscrossed, leaving holes for an animal's hoof to slip through.

We had a plan to go down a nearby trail that led to a hopefully dried-up bog that was usually impassable. Once across the bog, we could go through a gate and be on the other side of the cattle guard. It was exciting to think of finding new trails. My husband rode his new quarter horse named Vinny. Don't ask me why he called it that, but he liked the name.

All was good on the beginning trail. When we got close to the bog, my horse, Rocky, began to sink in the mire. Soon he was a foot deep and not too keen on going further. My husband, however, wasn't easily discouraged and he ventured on. We had chosen not to go across a nearby footbridge that had looked a little unsafe. Bad plan!

No sooner was Vinny in the wet bog than he sunk up to his chest. My husband had little experience with such predicaments. Rocky and I were watching from a distance and not budging at all. We saw the whole thing unfold before our eyes. Vinny was plum stuck. With a great effort, Vinny plunged forward, bursting the girth from his Australian saddle. Of course, my husband went off with the saddle right into the muck and mire. I tried not to laugh. He looked up to avoid Vinny's legs as Vinny managed to get out of the hole, leaving his rider behind.

I waited for Vinny to take off now that he was free of saddle and rider. Nope. My husband had one of the reins, so Vinny just stood quietly right at the edge of the mire. He wasn't daunted one bit. As a matter of fact, when my husband managed to stand up, holding the saddle and broken girth, Vinny continued to stand fast. I was really impressed with his manners. It told me that Vinny had a good mind during a moment of panic, that he was loyal to his rider and not about to take off down the road.

The real test came to Vinny when he was asked to go back through the mire the same way. My husband, with his cowboy boots full of water, had to walk ahead of Vinny through the deep sinking bog and hope Vinny would follow a good tug on the reins. Sure enough, Vinny crossed that bog one more time while sinking a second time up to his chest. I was real proud of that horse for not putting up an argument or taking off and shirking his responsibility to partner with his rider. Of course, I was real proud of my husband, too, for having the courage to get his horse back through the bog. That was the shortest ride we had ever been on. Both rider and horse were soaking wet and full of mud when they trudged home together, minus a little pride. Vinny was sure a prize horse.

This story presents a clear picture of standing firm in the middle of difficulty. Some people panic when they lose control. Others lose courage and give up. Vinny stood firm in the middle of the problem, waiting for his master's instructions. There is a Bible verse that gives us clear instruction about what to do during a time of trial:

> Finally, be strong in the Lord and in the strength of his might.
> Put on the whole armor of God, that you may be able
> to stand against the schemes of the devil...
> Therefore take up the whole armor of God,
> that you may be able to withstand in the evil day,
> and having done all, to stand firm.
>
> (Ephesians 6:10-11, 13)

Have you been in a battle or a difficult situation when you felt like giving up or running away? We all have. Take courage and stand firm in the armour of God, because God is mighty to save!

Can you name all the parts of God's armour and what they are for? The whole armour is a picture of Jesus. When you trust in Jesus, you are wearing that armour.

Try playing a combat game with a partner. You stand firm on one spot or in a circle and your partner tries to make you move from that spot by pushing and pulling, or tricking you off your spot. The stronger one usually wins the battle. God is stronger than Satan, so put your trust in God when Satan tries to get you off your stand for truth and righteousness.

Devotional Fifteen:
Turtle Mania!

WHEN WE MOVED TO OUR NEW HOBBY FARM, WE HAD THE wonderful blessing of enjoying a pond. Over the eight years of living there, our pond attracted many creatures of the day and night. At first glance, you might not notice any pond life, but standing on the edge provided a close-up view of frogs, water snakes, dragonflies, bees, tadpoles, small fish, and water skitters.

Our son bought a license to raise trout. He put twenty-five young trout in the pond. It didn't take long before a heron routinely swooped down to scoop a mouthful of delicious trout. We noticed a muskrat swimming around in search of those trout, too!

Often during our farm chores, we heard the familiar honking sound and loud splash of a pair of wandering wild ducks or Canada Geese. They would enjoy a brief swim and look about while en route to better ponds. We once saw a handsome kingfisher dive into the pond from one of the nearby willow trees.

A special pair of mallard ducks laid their eggs in the brush and reared their brood on the pond for a few years in a row. It was quite a spectacle when the proud mother and father ducks led their fine ducklings across the pond for their first sail. The mother was so careful to protect her young. She kept them hidden in the tall grass and undergrowth for most of the spring. When summer came, they disappeared.

The pond always got a rude awakening on a hot day when our overweight dog, Lady, waddled down the embankment to take a refreshing dip. She was the biggest show yet, disturbing the pond's perfect serenity. We enjoyed the pond so much that we placed a lovely wooden bench near its edge. It was our practice to sit with the dogs and watch life happen.

One dry, hot day, life on the pond changed. My cousin came by to drop off a critter she had found ambling along the road. She had rescued it from fatigue and predators. It was a very large slider turtle, about the size of a dinner plate. The turtle fascinated me. It was the perfect creature for our pond. She set the turtle on the grassy edge, and it knew exactly what to do. In an instant, it scurried down the grass slope into the pond and out of sight! That turtle was the highlight of our pond for four years. It was so shy that whenever the turtle sensed our presence, it vanished in a flash. The turtle had a habit of sunning every morning where the sun's rays were the warmest. Sometimes we could see it swimming across the pond or just floating, showing only its tiny head. It had a perfect resting spot on a mud shelf or tree root. Every day we greeted the turtle and watched it scamper back into the pond.

In early fall, the turtle hibernated in the deep mud until everything was warm again in the spring. It seemed happy on its own until one day I found it a long ways from the pond, near the horses. It was focused on digging in the dirt, trying to make a hole. That was the first time it didn't frighten back to the pond. I realized that the turtle was probably lonely and wanted a mate.

I asked the Lord to help me find a mate for it. It wasn't easy to find another turtle its own size. The pet stores only had tiny turtles and larger turtles were very expensive. I mulled the problem in my mind for quite a while until I simply forgot about the turtle, because we had a wedding reception to host for our daughter and son-in-law. After the wedding, I noticed that the turtle was gone. Not gone as in hibernation, since it was September, but gone for good! It had been like family, a familiar critter around the farm. We all missed that turtle so much. It didn't come back. I imagined it being terrorized by all the cacophony of the wedding and just packing up and leaving in a huff. Where was it? Was it safe? Would it come back?

In the late fall, about three months later, our farrier came over one day to shoe our horses' feet. That's when we got news of the turtle's whereabouts. The farrier routinely stepped down to the pond's edge to scoop a bucket of water to cool off the horseshoes before handling them.

"Where's the turtle?" he asked. Everyone who visited us was familiar with our turtle.

"Oh, it's disappeared," I said. "Ever since the wedding reception."

"Really? Well, I was just shoeing a horse the other day and the owner said he had a stray turtle come into his backyard from the forest. He promptly put the turtle in his bathtub and started caring for it by giving it raw meat."

"Could it be our turtle?" I asked in amazement.

We discussed what the turtle looked like. It sure sounded like our turtle. He commented that the turtle had teeth marks on it from an attacker, such as a dog. Our poor turtle! What had he gone through to journey several miles, cross a river, and tromp through thick forests with all kinds of danger lurking nearby?

We got the man's name and phone number who had the turtle and gave him a call. He described the turtle just as we knew it. We promptly drove twenty minutes to his home and viewed the turtle happily swimming in his bathtub. Yes, it looked like ours, but it was so friendly. I held it for a moment, noticing how tame it had become after living in their bathtub for two weeks and being handfed. He offered us the turtle back, so we put the turtle in a box and drove him home.

We were relieved to see it rescued a second time. Perhaps it had journeyed those three months in search of a long lost mate. We'll never know for sure, but we do know that it ended right back at the start, and for that we were happy. It was the prodigal turtle come home!

So we thought. We decided to name it Curtis, after the man who had rescued him. I felt bad for Curtis, because he had travelled so far and endured so much but didn't accomplish his goal of finding a mate.

Not long after, Curtis hibernated and all was quiet on the frozen pond. When spring arrived, we had the biggest shock. One warm spring day when I was driving past the pond, I happened to glance sideways, looking for Curtis, when I saw two turtles sunning side by side. One quickly disappeared and the other stayed put. He didn't seem the least bit frightened by our presence. Truth be told, the turtle that had disappeared was our turtle, and the one that wasn't shy was the newfound turtle from the man's bathtub. Now our turtle had a friend, maybe even a mate!

What a strange set of circumstances for God to put together in order for our turtle to find a mate. Even stranger still was the fact that after two weeks we only saw one turtle present on the shore by itself. Then, in time, there were no turtles on the shore. This is where the mystery ends. Both turtles only hung around the pond for a few months and then they were gone again! We'll never know the ending of this story. What's your guess?

There is much to learn from this ending. What did you learn? I learned that God is in control of all creation. He is the one who put the habit of hibernation into turtles, bears, frogs, groundhogs, and many other animals. God can do the impossible, even with turtles! I thought it was up to me to find a mate for our turtle, but God did it His way.

We often try to fix something our way even while praying for God to solve the problem. If we are patient to wait for God to move, we will be pleasantly surprised! God's ways are so different from our ways that we really need to expect the impossible and supernatural. Ask God to teach you His ways and live expecting God to do supernatural things to answer your prayers.

Do you remember the story of the five loaves and two fishes? Jesus really surprised His disciples by taking a few loaves and fishes from a boy and multiplying it to feed over five thousand people. The disciples were surprised again when Jesus did it a second time. Should we be surprised when God performs signs, wonders, and miracles? I don't think so. God is supernatural, so the supernatural workings of God should be a part of normal everyday Christian life. Set your sights on the God of the impossible. Mary, the mother of Jesus said, "For nothing will be impossible with God" (Luke 1:37).

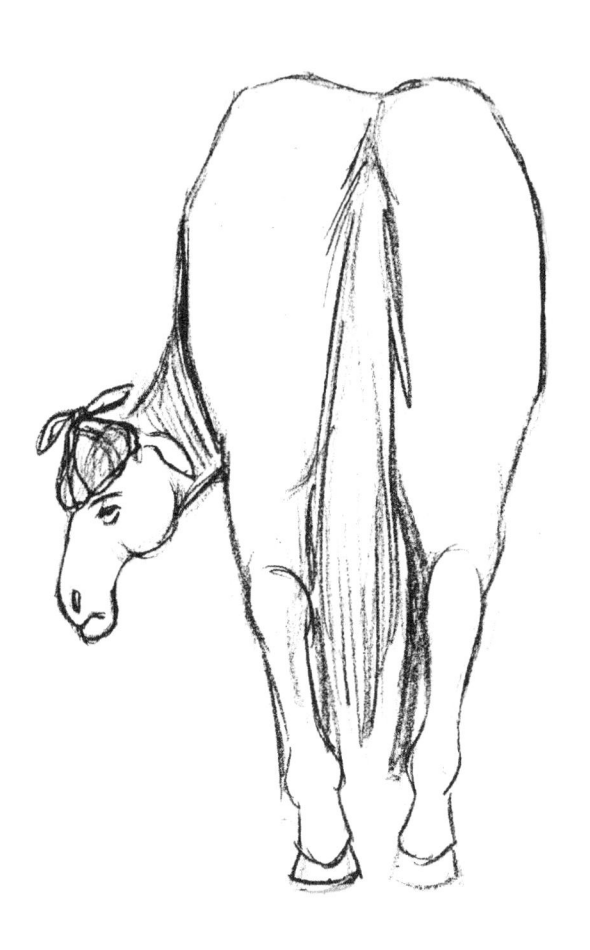

Devotional Sixteen:
Bloopers!

WHAT IS A BLOOPER? OUR FIRST WEEK LIVING IN THE Cariboo was quite a challenge. We wouldn't have survived if it wasn't for a little humour and all the family help. Life is full of bloopers, but we never would have imagined that so many mistake could happen in one week. We moved into our new house, put up a horse corral in three days, and finished the last nail on a rail when the horses arrived on the fourth morning. Grandpa had to return to work in a week, so we had little time to learn about our new machinery and attachments and get the hay in along with so many other tasks, not to mention eating and sleeping.

Grandpa was quite excited to work his new tractor and mower while cutting our first hay crop. It was early July and the ground was still wet in some of the pastures. Little did he realize when driving on the far lower pasture that his tractor wheels would sink so rapidly. In no time, he was stuck in the mire. Our faithful neighbour came to our rescue with his backhoe, but to no avail. He got stuck, too! Then they got big timbers to boost his machine up and move it onto safe dry ground. The next day they rounded up a hundred feet of chain from the neighbours to pull out the tractor with the backhoe. In the end, all was rescued, only time lost for haying. One good discovery was that the soil was a real nice rich black, great for farming!

When he finally started mowing, the large tire on the cutter went flat, so my husband had a big delay in getting a new one. Our neighbour, Henry, came to the rescue with a tire that he drilled holes in to make it fit.

Grandpa and I both lost our sunglasses while mowing the hay. When we put things down, they would disappear into the cut hay, never to be found again. I also lost a good set of earrings when boosting my granddaughter up on my shoulders to check on the haying operations. Grandpa drove over his thermos when moving the tractor through the gate. Not to mention, the mower almost took off my leg as I stood by the gate to check to see if there was enough room for us to drive through it.

Grandpa backed up the hay truck into the wire cable which ran from the barn to the house. That took a while to repair. I damaged my very expensive rowing shell while backing up my car and forgetting that the boat was on the car rack. The boat suffered only a mild buckling in the middle and the house was fine.

We drove a flat deck farm truck that had almost no brake power and it wouldn't start when needed to pick up the bales of hay. We jump-started it many times and let it sit when flooded with gas. We prayed over it and did whatever was necessary to get it rumbling down the driveway to fetch the hay bales.

Our new cable and internet wouldn't work and our house plumbing had two leaks. Our telephone wouldn't work because one of the number pads got stuck and made phoning impossible.

One day, I heard a *clop-clop* sound on the top of the barn where the hay bales would eventually be stored. The two horses had wandered onto the loft and peered over the end, looking down several feet to the ground. I gasped and ran to shoo them away from the edge before either one fell off. We promptly rigged up a barrier to avoid future accidents.

When we had one field divided in lovely windrows, a strange wind came along in the form of a funnel and swept the hay high into the air, making quite a mess. Getting the hay in was a real chore. Each time we tried to bale the hay, a thunderstorm came, so the hay had to be turned the next day. This happened several times. Our neighbour coached us on how to wait until the hay was real dry before we baled. It was a game of cat and mouse. Out came the sun and dried up the hay, then down poured the rain, spoiling our baling chances. Eventually we got most of our hay in, but then it was time for Grandpa to leave and go back to work on Vancouver Island before we were finished. Fortunately, our two neighbours came over with their machinery and finished up the mowing and baling while my daughter and grandsons helped me to get in the remaining 250 bales.

It was a comical first week on the farm, but we weren't going to be easily discouraged just because we were greenhorns. Since that first week of moving in to our new farm, we have had many more bloopers, such as our horse having colic three times. Grandpa's horse once tried to escape under the gate rails, and another time he smashed right through three rails to get to his hay.

Bloopers, or mistakes, are a part of experiencing new life challenges and taking risks so we can experience more of God's grace. If we let those bloopers get us down, discouraged, angry, or frustrated, then they win the battle. Learn from every mistake or failure and use them for good. Every day is a new day and we don't think about what bloopers will happen next, we think about the blessings God will bring our way to overshadow the difficulties.

King David made some pretty big mistakes, but he learned from them and didn't give up on the plans God had for him as king.

All of these bloopers remind me of how Satan tries to bring discouragement into our lives. Psalm 23 is a journey that God takes us on in good times and difficult times, but in the end, surely goodness and mercy will follow us all the days of our life. God is with you through all your bloopers, so just trust Him to turn each one out for good and not for evil. God is for you, cheering you on through all life's challenges. Shake off the mistakes and take hold of the next adventure God has waiting for you.

And we know that for those who love God all things work together for good,
for those who are called according to his purpose.

(Romans 8:28)

Devotional Seventeen:
Cougar Scare

WE SPENT CHRISTMAS DAY WITH MOST OF OUR FAMILY AT our home in the Cariboo. It turned out to be quite the scare. We had our traditional crepe brunch with dollops of whipped cream, bowls of various fresh fruit, and streams of maple syrup. After our feast, everyone bundled up for a walk to our favourite hill where we could launch our sleds down the winding path. Our son-in-law went ahead of us to make a sled path by driving the snowmobile up and down the slope. It was the perfect day, the sun glistening on a foot and a half of fluffy snow for an afternoon to frolic with our grandchildren.

Of course, what would any adventure be unless the five family dogs came, too? They bounded ahead of us with much barking and fanfare. Annie was the first up the sled hill. I was the next one, running up behind her. Suddenly, we heard a series of painful cries from Annie in the woods. We all stopped and listened. Annie often came upon wildlife and would yip and yap for a while, announcing her discovery. But this time it was not a yip or yap, it was a series of mournful yelps of distress. I leaped into action, panicking inside. Was this the end for Annie? Just before entering the forest, Annie came darting out with streams of blood falling into the snow. I noticed that her neck was smeared in blood. In terror, she fled across the path and disappeared into the forest toward home. Yes, she was alive, but obviously injured.

My daughter caught up with me and we went into the woods, searching for the predator. The trail of blood led us to many deer tracks and to the place of attack. Our son came to check out the situation and he discovered cougar tracks nearby. I raced home to check on Annie, knowing full well that she would head home for help. The blood drops took me home. My husband got home ahead of me. He had Annie penned in the laundry room to keep her quiet. My help was needed to apply pressure to her wounds. Together we tried to stop the flow of blood under Annie's neck and belly. There were two gashes from the cougar's claws and numerous other minor claw marks on her back and rump.

It wasn't long before all the family returned. No one felt much like sledding after that scary incident. How dare a cougar stay hidden in the trees, ready to launch on some poor unsuspecting victim, such as Annie? We all realized that it could have been one of the grandkids. Our son tracked the cougar with his dog, Timber, for a few kilometres and then he gave up on catching that smart cat. It was the second time in a week that the cougar was spotted in our area.

Annie's throat was very swollen and painful, so it was hard for her to eat or swallow for a few days. She barely had enough energy to move. She stood for long periods just swaying back and forth, with her head hanging low like she was ready to collapse in a heap. She couldn't lie down easily because of her wounds. After four days of quiet and drinking turkey gravy in warm water, Annie recovered quite well. She didn't have stitches or veterinary care, but she did have prayer.

Our prayers were answered, because there was no infection from the cougar's claws. Annie wanted to go outside, and when we finally let her out, she didn't wander far or stay out long. Two weeks later, we could hear Annie's familiar yip and yap when she cornered a bird or squirrel. The cougar scare slowed Annie to a stop, but only for a short while. I hoped and prayed that Annie would continue to stay safe as she frolicked and romped in the hayfields and surrounding forests.

I sure hope Annie is wiser about predators from now on. We want her to continue doing what God created her for, to enjoy hunting in the wide open spaces and not be fearful of having new adventures.

I'm sure that you have heard of sad stories where someone was hurt, and perhaps even killed. The Apostle Paul never stopped sharing about Jesus with people, even when it got him into trouble. He knew that God was with him, so he took great joy and courage in doing God's will. Don't let fear or bad things hold you back from serving God or following His will in your life.

The enemy, Satan, is lurking around like a roaring lion, seeing who he can devour. Be wise and learn to listen to God's voice of guidance, encouragement, and love.

> Look carefully then how you walk, not as unwise but as wise, making the best use of the time, because the days are evil. Therefore do not be foolish, but understand what the will of the Lord is.
>
> (Ephesians 5:15-17)

Devotional Eighteen:
Lowly Donkey

TODAY WAS THE DAY TO ADD A NEW PET TO OUR ENTOURAGE of farm animals we have owned over the past thirty-five years. I didn't rush into this decision, but carefully weighed the pros and cons of having a donkey. When I saw a miniature donkey for sale in the local newspaper, I jumped at the opportunity to have our very own. We made a bargain with the owners to barter hay for the donkey, and in two days the donkey arrived on our property in a large horse trailer. It took two people to push the donkey out and one to pull him in the right direction. They pulled his ears and lifted his tail to move him forward when he braced hard. He skidded on all four straight legs right into his new home. His fur reminded me of a cuddly koala bear, his ears were very large like a mule, and his head was framed by mounds of fur. Yes, he was strange-looking, but oh so sweet, a bundle of affection.

I'm used to horses acting out when they're introduced to new surroundings and people, but there was no drama from our new donkey. I gave him a few thin slices of carrot for a friendship offering. His muzzle slowly worked each carrot slice into his mouth as he discovered the taste of new food. He was shy and lowly in manner. It took a week of studying this curious pet before we came up with a name. The rhyme "Georgie Porgie kissed the girls and made them cry" came to mind. It suited our romantic little fellow. Once Georgie knew you could be trusted, he was willing to come in close and give you a little kiss. How adorable is that?

Every day I planned to spend time with our sweet donkey. He wouldn't come to me or let me in his space until I proved myself gentle and trustworthy. If my hand moved too quickly, he would run away. If I approached too quickly, he would run away. Georgie demanded respect and lots of patience and gentleness, or it was a no-go. I would approach him slowly and quietly, in a low position, finishing near him on my knees. When he was ready, he would come over very slowly, just close enough for me to reach out and give him a scratch. He would come closer after each scratch, edging his way to my heart. Every day we would repeat the ritual until he was standing right up against me, practically in my face. He loved a big scratch all over his furry body. His fur was so thick that I had to concentrate on getting my fingers underneath it. I loved Georgie from the moment I laid eyes on him. He was a winner with us!

Why did I get Georgie? Well, maybe the question should be why God sent Georgie to us. I think God has a lot to do with Georgie being at our home. Georgie is a picture of humility and grace. He loves relationships with people who are gentle, kind, and trustworthy, and who respect him as a worthy friend. Georgie's personality has a lot to offer anyone who wants to be his friend. He stands humbly with his head down and meekly waits for permission to come. He is not forceful, rude, or arrogant. He can be trusted. I believe Georgie is one of the noblest creatures God created. Jesus chose to ride on a young colt, or donkey, when he came into Jerusalem as King of the Jews. Jesus chose a creature of humility and nobility like himself. It is a strange combination, but very much God. I have a lot to learn from Georgie.

Despite Georgie being just shy of three feet high, donkeys have a reputation to face their enemies, to fight and not run. Our fearsome little donkey has a bray that makes your heart turn as he greets you at feeding time, beseeching your mercy.

Jesus said that unless we humble ourselves as a little child, we cannot enter the kingdom of heaven. He also says that humility shows great strength, because God resists the proud but gives grace or strength to the humble. The donkey is a humble burden-bearer of great strength that often carries heavy loads for poor people who cannot afford anything else. Jesus, strong and mighty, humbly invites us to give Him all of our burdens and He will carry them for us.

> Come to me, all who labor and are heavy laden, and I will give you rest. Take my yoke upon you, and learn from me, for I am gentle and lowly in heart, and you will find rest for your souls. For my yoke is easy, and my burden is light.
>
> (Matthew 11:28-30)

One example of humility is making other people feel more important than you, when you lift them up higher than yourself by speaking kind and encouraging words and by showing friendship and honour towards them. Think of people in your life who you can be an example to—your parents, siblings, friends, and strangers.

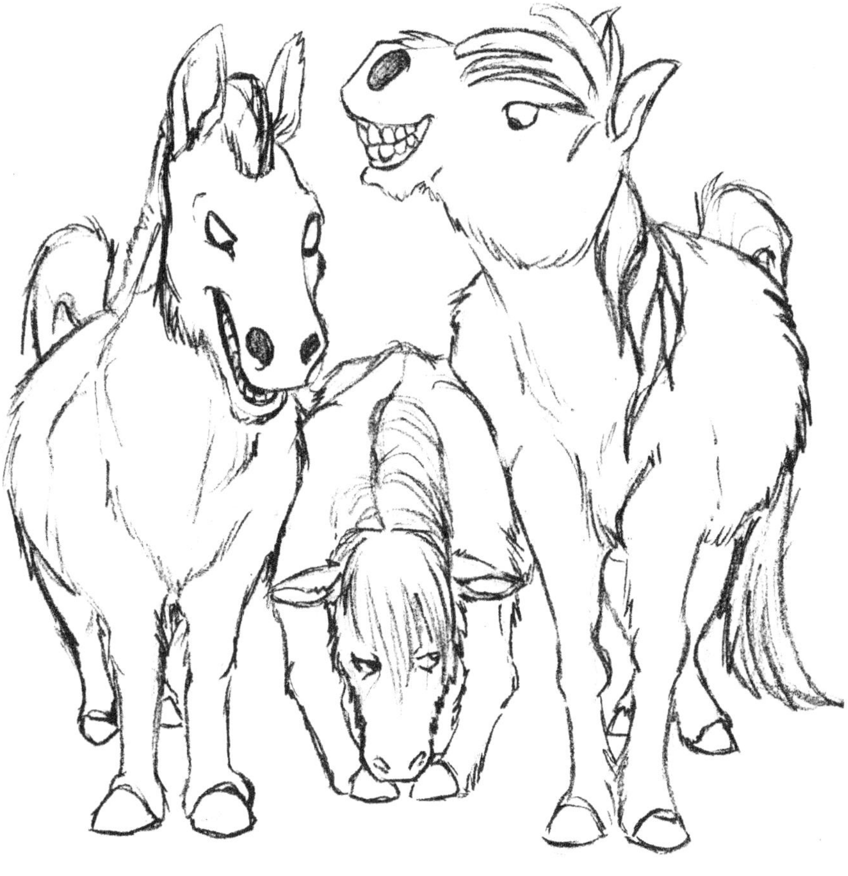

Devotional Nineteen:
Challenging Charlie

AFTER A FEW DAYS OF WATCHING HUMBLE GEORGIE SETTLE into his new home, I observed how lonely he was. He stood close to the fence so he could see the three horses nearby. They were as intrigued by him as he was by them. It was decided that we would add one more animal to the mix so Georgie would have a buddy to hang out with. Now that we were grandparents, we loved to take our grandchildren riding. We felt it was appropriate to get a pony. A Welsh pony came to mind. I didn't realize that there were several classes of Welsh ponies, from very small size to horse size.

Off we went to a farm that raised Welsh ponies. There were two particular ponies that were just the size we wanted, a dappled grey and a chestnut. We decided on the one-and-a-half-year-old dappled grey pony. It was a little bigger than Georgie.

The pony was very alert, with dark, round, and intense eyes that zoomed in on every movement. His long, scraggly mane and tail needed a good grooming and his fur was as thick as a Persian rug. He was a delight to look at, compact and lively. I noticed that the pony wasn't happy in his very tight pen because of two bigger ponies that ruled the roost over him. He was constantly moving to escape their bullying.

   I felt sorry for him and wanted to give him a better home. I felt that because the pony and Georgie were both boys, they should get along just fine. Fortunately, we could pay for the pony by trading next summer's hay. The deal was settled and the pony was ours! That afternoon, the pony was trailered to its new home. I was so excited to have this sweet little pony as a companion for Georgie.

   Georgie was in for a big surprise, and so were we. Our new pony pranced into the corral and took over immediately. He was now the bigshot at the top of the pecking order. It didn't take long for us to name the smart pony Charlie, which sounded wonderful when calling out to him every feeding. My granddaughter always spoke affectionately about her cousin, named Charlee, and so I thought Charlie was a good name.

After a few weeks of Georgie being bossed around by Charlie, something happened. The donkey decided it was time to draw some boundaries. One day, I witnessed Georgie giving Charlie a good boot, and on another day I noticed two good patches of fur missing from Charlie's neck and side. Yes, Georgie was no pushover. He wasn't going to put up with a fancy pony that had no manners or respect for the lowly and meek creature that he was.

Charlie and Georgie really began to bond with each other. One sunny day, they could be seen grooming each other and interlocking their necks in a friendly fashion. Georgie would bite and massage Charlie's withers with his teeth, and in return Charlie would do the same. It was a real exchange of friendship. All barriers had broken down, with no bossing or lording it over by Charlie. This behaviour went on for quite some time before they each got a little worn out.

Charlie will sometimes show off his zest for life by sprinting from one end of the corral to the other. He races so fast that he falls into the snow, flipping over onto his side or back. But he's always back on his feet in a jiffy. Georgie doesn't agree with Charlie's antics sometimes, so he'll move off behind a tree to tend to his itches and untidy fur. When Charlie is all done, there's peace in the corral again, much to Georgie's delight.

I'm so glad that we got Charlie, even though he's a little bossy with Georgie. They are bonding well and becoming best friends.

What is God showing you about Charlie and Georgie's friendship? It didn't start off well, but in time the two learned to appreciate each other. Georgie had to set good boundaries with Charlie or he would have got picked on all the time. Georgie knows when to take a break from Charlie, and Charlie has learned to respect Georgie's space. I like how the two have worked out their relationship. We can show God's love to people even when they don't treat us well. We may not always get along or be compatible with the people in our lives, but we do need to respect them. In time, if we are patient and caring, we may win them over as friends.

Do you know of friendships in the Bible that are special between two people? There's the friendship of Jonathan and David and the friendship of Ruth and Naomi, who came from different backgrounds but became loyal to each other. God wants you to have good friends all through your life. Good friends are precious, so thank God for the ones you have and work at being a good friend to them. Ephesians 4:32 says it very well: "Be kind to one another, tenderhearted, forgiving one another, as God in Christ forgave you."

Devotional Twenty:
Trusting Charlie

DO YOU KNOW WHAT "SKITTERY" MEANS? IT'S NOT IN THE dictionary, but it's a word that best describes Charlie, our Welsh pony. He's like a hotwire dancing on a rooftop, or like a Mexican jumping bean in your hand, or like a hopping sand flea. Charlie is always reacting and moving because he just doesn't trust anyone or anything, except Georgie. At least, I thought so.

From the day Charlie arrived, he wouldn't let you come within ten feet of him. If you tried to touch him, he would react like a dog that got stung by a bee. Over time, with quietness, gentleness, patience, and daily routine, Charlie would stretch out his neck to touch me on the hand and begin licking. If I moved even a hair, he was gone, often falling over backwards! I needed to come up with a method of catching Charlie so I could begin the process of grooming, checking him over for problems, getting him ready for the farrier to trim his hooves and for training to pull a cart. I had never owned an animal so nervous and jumpy.

It was going to require much diligence on my part to win the next level of Charlie's trust and affection. I was up for the challenge, and so was Charlie! With some help, I was able to manoeuvre him into the barn where he could find his bucket with a small handful of oats. He wouldn't take carrots or apples, so we had to give him oats, which unfortunately were very high in energy, causing Charlie to sometimes bounce around the paddock. Once Charlie was lured into the barn, we slid some skinny poles across the entrance to keep him from running out. When I slowly climbed over the poles to join Charlie, he began shaking something awful. Just touching Charlie seemed painful to him.

Every feeding time, I reached out to him in gentleness. The first time I tried to approach Charlie in the shelter, he scrambled around me and jumped straight up and over the poles. In a flash, he was gone. Wow, what an athlete! He had cleared a bar that was higher than him. Such a robust pony!

Finally, one day, I was able to slip the lead rope around his neck and place the halter ever so slowly over his nose. Charlie seemed spellbound whenever I made contact with him. He wanted to run away, but he couldn't get past me to jump out. I tried to leave the rope long and loose so he wouldn't feel held against his will. We had slow progress. Charlie would let me lead him around the large corral, with intermittent stops where I had to give gentle tugs and then let go so he would want to come forward and follow the feel. Sometimes Charlie would revert back to his nervous and jittery self, falling over in a mad scramble to get away. He often expected the worst.

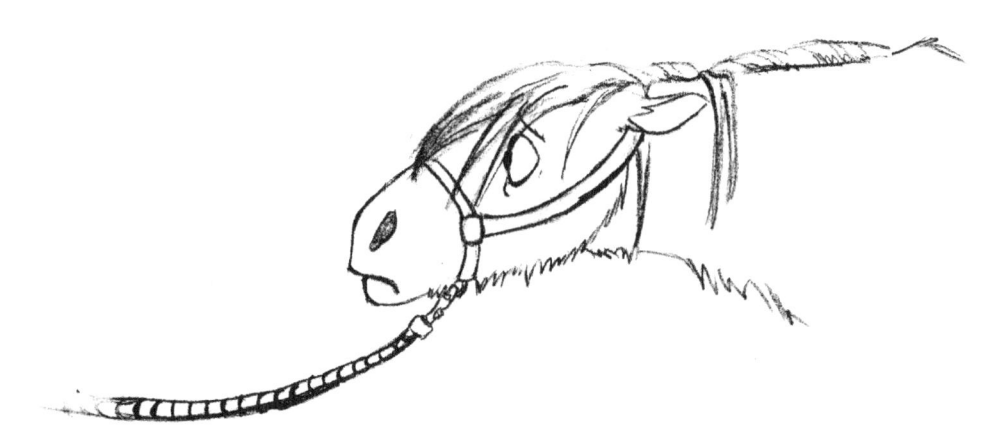

Amazing things do happen when we least expect them. One day, after feeding the horses their grain, I looked over at Charlie and Georgie in their paddock. I had to walk closer to make sure I was seeing right: two large ravens were sitting on Charlie's rump. They were pecking continuously at him! What was Charlie doing about that? Well, he was thoroughly enjoying every peck. His head was stretched out and his mouth moved in rhythm with each peck, and each peck drew up a tuft of fluff from Charlie's fur. Soon the ravens' beaks were overloaded with fluff to the point of gagging themselves. How funny is that? I waited for the comedy act to end, but the ravens and Charlie danced to their own tune, unaware of anything else. I'm not sure how those ravens communicated with Charlie that they wanted to sit on his rump to collect some fluff and give him those much-needed love pecks. Charlie was sure convinced of their good intentions.

Can you learn something from this funny story? Some people are just like Charlie. They don't trust people. They run away when they're afraid. They worry about the smallest things and live in their own shy and lonely world. But there is One who's greater, stronger, and more passionate to save the fearful, hurting, and lonely.

God's plan is to win people over who are like Charlie. He does it with amazing love, gentleness, patience, and understanding. When the time is right, God tugs on that person's heart and He wins them over in a way that they are changed forever. Walls of fear and lies that kept them apart come down and there is a joyous meeting of two friends, like the ravens and Charlie.

Oh, taste and see that the Lord is good!

(Psalm 34:8)

Devotional Twenty-One:
Wipeout!

ONE OF MY DREAMS FOR RAISING OUR CHILDREN WAS TO have a hobby farm in the country. Farm life has a way of teaching children about responsibility, work ethic, and a love for animals and the great outdoors. When my husband and I bought our first home, we made sure it was an acreage so we could learn how to raise and care for animals before we had children. We had ducks, chickens, horses, a dog, a cat, and goats. We lost those goats because we didn't realize that goats should never be tethered in an area where they can get tangled. Several years later, our children raised goats, but they lost them, too. Then we raised goats for milk until the mother goat lost all three of her babies during a complicated birth, and in the end she died as well.

For thirty-three years, we suffered much discouragement from losing many of our wonderful pets and farm animals to predators and mishaps. Despite all our losses, we never gave up having animals, because the rewards of caring for them and sharing them with our family and friends far outweighed the burden of loss.

Our biggest animal loss happened when our remaining Muscovy duck was sitting on the many eggs she laid under the chicken coop. We were so excited to have ducklings on the farm, especially since we had a large pond. After what seemed like an eternity, thirteen ducklings appeared, one by one. Every day the mother paraded her ducklings proudly over the acreage, taking them for swims in the pond and visiting us near the house. She knew to hide them under her body when they were resting.

We knew to put them under the chicken coop and lock them in every night.

When I collected the chicken eggs from the coop each morning, I did a count of the ducklings. It's normal to lose some to predators, such as hawks, eagles, owls, mink, rats, and perhaps the overzealous family dog. That's exactly what happened. Sometimes, while picking up horse manure, I would find a dead duckling in the pasture. Each day another duckling mysteriously disappeared until there was only one left.

I was so worried for that last duckling. I felt pity for the mother duck, who had worked hard to hatch them into the world and then try to protect them from sly predators. Sure enough, the last of the thirteen ducklings disappeared and that was that! Off the mother duck waddled to the pond to enjoy a leisurely sv knowing she had done her best and was now free of her daily burdens.

It seems cruel to lose all the ducklings in such a short time span, perhaps two weeks. They were tiny and vulnerable in the big wide open spaces where their mother took them to find insects and other food. I'm sure she would start all over again next spring to raise another brood. We weren't going to risk keeping her over the winter and see her eaten, too! All of our Indian Runner ducks and other mature Muscovy ducks had been attacked and died that year, a total of fourteen fowl.

A plan formed in my mind to save the mother duck. My friend lived down the road and she loved to take in orphan critters. I made a quick visit to her farm, and soon our mommy Muscovy moved into a miniature penthouse suite with a pond view and many farm friends. Wild ducks stopped at the pond daily to get their free feeding. Two geese lived there, too, along with horses, cows, and miniature donkeys. Mother Muscovy had lots of company, the best food, and a safe place to live. I went back two years later to visit her and she was still enjoying the best life possible.

You might be sad right now, or you might be asking the question, "What can we learn from all this discouraging news of losing so many ducklings?" We can learn why there is death and suffering in this world. Does God care?

Mother Muscovy's story reminds me of another sad story with a good ending. The Bible tells us of the greatest loss and discouragement in history. In the Garden of Eden, Adam and Eve walked and talked with God. Life was perfect and wonderful. Adam gave names to all the animals God brought him. There was no death, disease, or sorrow for Adam and Eve or any of the animals, until one day when Satan came in the form of a serpent. He came to rob, kill, and destroy all the good that God made. He first deceived Eve by tempting her to disobey God's only command, not to eat from the Tree of the Knowledge of Good and Evil. Eve chose to take the fruit and give some to Adam. Sin came into the world through their disobedience to God. All mankind and creation fell from God's glory and was cursed. Nothing and no one is perfect now. Man's first sin brought death, disease, sorrow, shame, guilt, and tears into the world.

That's not the end of the story, though. God had a perfect plan to take away the power of sin and death in the world and bring man back into relationship with Him. John 3:16 says, "For God so loved the world, that he gave his only Son, that whoever believes in him should not perish but have eternal life." Rejoice and be encouraged by this good news! An even better day will come soon. Jesus will come a second time and take us up to be with Him forever in heaven. Then all of God's creation will be new again, just like in the beginning.

Suffering and death were never part of God's original plan for mankind and His creation. God made us, the little ducklings, and all creation to glorify Him forever.

> For the wages of sin is death, but the free gift of God
> is eternal life in Christ Jesus our Lord.
>
> (Romans 6:23)

This story may focus on loss and discouragement, but the conclusion is about encouragement not only in your future in heaven, but for living right now! God is in control of your life. You can give Him all your cares and heavy burdens, for He cares for you. Your prayers matter to God and He hears every one of them. He sees all your tears and knows all your thoughts. He has promised to never leave you or forsake you. He has given you a wonderful inheritance of being adopted into his family, so you can call him Daddy. You have a rich inheritance from your Daddy to enjoy all His goodness, love and, blessings now, despite the sad and evil happenings around you.

Devotional Twenty-Two:
Pure Joy

EVERY SPRING IN THE CARIBOO, I'M REMINDED OF THE PURE joy of just being alive and well. When the last snow finally melts, we all breathe a sigh of relief. Tufts of green emerald grass spring up through a maze of happy dandelions. All the earth trumpets God's mercy and grace. It is a blessed time of year when abundance flows, and sometimes overflows! Joyous symphonic sounds so glorious to the senses hold me spellbound by their never-ending praises and thanks to God.

Our dog Annie hibernates until spring. She spends most of her dull winter days indoors, snoozing, snoring, and sprawled out on her cushioned bed by the woodstove. Winter is fattening-up time for Annie. The Cariboo winter is too cold for her thin white coat and lean body. When temperatures plunge to −15°C or colder, Annie has to be pushed outside to relieve herself, which she does very quickly.

But come spring, Annie is a changed dog! Her familiar trademark is a broad grin on her face while on the run. It's like someone let her free after months of being cooped up. Her athletic body springs into action. The familiar buzz of bees, twitter of birds, and chatter of squirrels stirs all of Annie's senses into a joyous celebration that the hunt is on!

One day, I drove home down our long winding road and noticed Annie pouncing around in our neighbour's hayfield. I had to stop the car and watch her demonstration of pure joy. She was having the time of her life hunting for birds and mice. She ran in circles for a long time like a mad dog pursuing nothing. Most of her time was spent suspended in the air, trying to see her way through the tall grass. Every few moments, she would yip and yap with pure glee, reminding the world that she was strong and free and excited to live life again as a hunting dog should.

Georgie demonstrated similar joy when she—yes, it turned out our he-donkey was actually a she-donkey all along—was let out on the fresh spring grass for the first time. Georgie turned into a wind-up toy that was let go. No one could lead her anywhere. When the gate was opened, she raced onto the pasture as fast as her tiny legs could carry her, swinging her tail and doing circles and jumps. Her gymnastics were amazing as he showed off poetic leaps, side-kicks, and bucks all in one. I was holding her companion pony by a lead rope so we wouldn't have a collision of antics. Georgie ran right for us, leaping over the rope without incident. There was no holding her back, not even the temptation of munching on long-awaited sweet spring grass. Georgie brought laughter and joy to my heart that day. Never had I seen a creature release such great bursts of energy and speed. Watch out for Georgie!

Annie and Georgie both displayed a passion that is contagious. Their zeal reminds me of fireworks on a starry night, a waterfall gushing out of a rocky mountain top, or a shout echoing in a valley. Everyone goes "Ooh" and "Aah" at the sights and sounds.

Joy is like that. Joy is one of the fruits of the Holy Spirit, which God produces when you delight in Him. Annie and Georgie are both examples of pure joy. God wants you to have that kind of joy every day you live for Him. *"In Him we live and move and have our being"* (Acts 17:28).

The opposite of joy is sadness. Sadness makes you look down and feel hopeless and miserable. You don't want those kinds of feelings. The joy of the Lord is like medicine, pumping you full of God's goodness and grace so you can love others the way God loves you.

Enjoy reading the verses below and pick out one to memorize. Let the verse bring joy to your heart.

> And do not be grieved, for the joy of the Lord is your strength.
>
> (Nehemiah 8:10)

> Shout for joy to God, all the earth; sing the glory of his name;
> give to him glorious praise!
>
> (Psalm 66:1-2)

> For you shall go out in joy and be led forth in peace;
> the mountains and the hills before you shall break forth into singing,
> and all the trees of the field shall clap their hands.
>
> (Isaiah 55:12)

These things I have spoken to you,
that my joy may be in you, and that your joy may be full.

(John 15:11)

You make known to me the path of life; in your presence there is fullness of joy; at your right hand are pleasures forevermore.

(Psalm 16:11)

Devotional Twenty-Three:
Teamwork

ANGEL IS THE BOSS AROUND THE RANCH. DURING THE COLD winter months, she spends most of her time curled up in a snug and warm place indoors. But come spring, summer, and fall, she's a full-time huntress. We have many acres of hayfields where she spends her time patiently waiting for a field mouse to scurry out of its hole and stray into her path. She's an expert at catching birds, mice, and chipmunks.

When she catches a field mouse, she brings her prize quickly to the backyard where Timber is usually lazing on the porch or playing with Lady. Timber notices Angel has a live mouse hanging out of her mouth and waits for her to drop it at his feet. He picks up the mouse and plays with it while Kitty sits quietly. Timber sets his huge paws on the mouse, then bats the mouse into motion once again, only to knock it down for the umpteenth time, until the mouse falls over lifeless. Lady has been waiting very patiently nearby. When she sees the mouse is dead and that Timber has walked away, looking for another challenge, Lady moves in for the meal. She picks up the mouse, and with a chomp the mouse is finished.

The three critters—Angel, Timber, and Lady—work together as a team, each playing their part from start to finish. The first time I saw this, we had three visitors with us. They were horrified at the trauma of the poor mouse. We wanted to rescue the mouse, but it didn't seem fair to take away Angel's prize, spoil Timber's fun, and rob Lady of her meal. It was all so innocent and natural to them, but shocking to us!

I tried to see the positive side of their accomplishments. It was a picture of teamwork. Each one had a special role to play and each one shared in the prize. There was no fighting, no jealousy, or harassment in getting the mouse for themselves. Angel had it all figured out ahead of time and she let everyone in on her game.

God says in Proverbs 6:6 that we should study ants to see how hard they work as a team, and yet they have no leader to organize them. There is harmony and peace in their teamwork. Teamwork is also like watching a relay, where each runner passes a baton to the next runner until the final runner crosses the finish line. God says we have been given many gifts to build each other up in our faith. When we work together in unity and harmony, we produce a beautiful picture of fellowship in the Lord. Psalm 133:1–3 says,

> Behold, how good and pleasant it is when brothers [and sisters] dwell in unity! It is like the precious oil on the head, running down on the beard, on the beard of Aaron, running down on the collar of his robes! It is like the dew of Hermon, which falls on the mountains of Zion! For there the Lord has commanded the blessing, life forevermore.

This verse paints a picture of abundance and blessing in God. Satan wants to get our focus off unity and peace in teamwork, and instead stir up fighting, arguments, selfishness, jealousy, and greed with one another so we cannot accomplish much for Jesus. Remember the story of Angel, Timber, and Lady and work as a cooperative team for God's glory.

Devotional Twenty-Four:
God's Grace

I HAVE LOVED HORSES SINCE I WAS VERY YOUNG, MAYBE three years old. Most children love horses, unless they've had a bad experience. Falling off a horse, getting kicked, bitten, and stepped on numerous times didn't seem to keep me from wanting to get back on again. However, there was one particular horse, Rocky, who changed my way of thinking.

My friend Margaret and I were all set to go for our weekly trail ride in the nearby forest. Rocky was my big Tennessee walking horse, black and beautiful. He recently had a bad sense about the saddle on his back and decided to buck every time I tightened the saddle on him. It seemed that if I let Rocky buck for a little bit after the saddle was put on, he would settle down and let me ride him without any problems. This became a necessary routine if I wanted to ride safely. Rocky never used to be this way—that is, until a mysterious incident set him to fearing the saddle and pressure around his belly.

My memory of that awful day is still very real. I reached up to grab Rocky's curly black mane while placing my toe carefully into the stirrup. With a light and quick hop, I came to stand in the one stirrup, waiting to see if Rocky would move forward or stay quietly. He seemed a little edgy, but I didn't worry about it and sat down lightly on the saddle. Before I could pick up the reins or get my other foot into the stirrup, Rocky puffed out with a great surge of power and shot upward, hopping around like a pogo stick. On the first buck, I tried hanging onto his neck. Each buck sent me higher into the air until I was completely unglued from

Rocky and hanging to his neck. The third buck sent me flying helpless to the ground with a mighty thud. Disaster struck when my legs became entangled in the reins. When I was under Rocky's belly, he kept hopping over me.

My friend told me later that she had thought Rocky's feet were all over my body, but in fact I never felt a hoof on me. It took all my strength to rip the reins away from my legs so I could roll out from under him. When I did come loose, Rocky bucked away from me a short distance. He soon stood still, his head drooped low, waiting for me to take the saddle off.

My son Andrew came running from nearby to see my very still body lying motionless on the hard gravel driveway. Then my little girl, Grace, also came to my side and asked worriedly, "Are you going to die, Mommy?" I weakly asked my son to phone my prayer partner and the ambulance.

In a short while, an ambulance crew put me on a flat board to take me to the hospital. The doctor checked me all over with x-rays, but amazingly there were no broken bones, only deep bruising of the bones and muscles. I went home and spent a few days in bed recovering.

From that time on, I could no longer trust Rocky. When I stood beside him with the saddle in hand, we would both shake inside. He wouldn't let me saddle him and I was too fearful to ride him. Fear was now my greatest enemy. Riding Rocky was impossible if I wanted to stay safe. Rocky had scared everyone, including my family. He became very intimidating, fearful, and strongly independent. After much praying and asking God for a solution, I came to the conclusion that I couldn't put Rocky down, I couldn't sell him, and I couldn't ride him, but I could keep him around and hope for change.

One day, change did come my way. When a neighbour heard about my fall, she told me about a horse trainer who was very successful with healing riders and their horses. God sent me a lady who helped Rocky and me to face our fears and get back in the saddle. I was willing to trust God and let this woman teach me how to join up with Rocky and capture his heart and desire. When I chose to trust in God for the next four years of training, I experienced His grace sweeping away all my fears. Letting go of my fear of falling was very hard, but I chose to overcome my fears by listening to God instead of the lies of Satan. If I had never fallen off Rocky, I would never have learned so powerfully about God's grace. God has worked out all things for His glory. I am forever grateful to my Heavenly Father for showing me His gentleness and patience so I could win Rocky's trust and respect. It is now fourteen years later, and Rocky and I are great partners on the riding trails again, and I have never fallen off!

Have you ever had a bad incident in your life that made you fearful? If you have, then it's time to be rid of those negative fears.

Fear is like a trap that holds you captive. You become a slave to your fearful thoughts. Fear will control your life if you let it. Jesus loves you and He wants you to be happy and free from all fears. Put your trust in Jesus' love and care for you. He's the only one who can set you free and give you His perfect peace. Next time you have a fear attack, take a stand against the enemy of fear and command it to go away in the name and authority of Jesus. The Prince of Peace said to Joshua, and He says the same to you, "Have I not commanded you? Be strong and courageous. Do not be frightened, and do not be dismayed, for the Lord your God is with you wherever you go" (Joshua 1:9). Speak these words out loud when fear attacks you.

There is no fear in love, but perfect love casts out fear.

(1 John 4:18)

Peace I leave with you; my peace I give to you. Not as the world gives do I give to you. Let not your hearts be troubled, neither let them be afraid.

(John 14:27)

Devotional Twenty-Five:
Visitor

WINTER IN THE CARIBOO ALWAYS HAS A FEW VERY COLD days that keep most people indoors. While driving up our long driveway one day, I thought of the helpless creatures trying to stay warm and find food in the deep snow. I prayed silently, "God, please show me any critters that are struggling to stay alive that might need my help." I was reminded to set up the bird feeder with seed for the few remaining birds. We usually did put a feeder out, but this winter we forgot.

God had another needy animal in mind for us to help. When I drove behind our house, I noticed a quick movement cross the horse paddock. It was a large domestic cat making its way to the top of the barn. Suddenly, the cat disappeared into the hay bales. Later at night, Grandpa went out to feed the horses and I asked him to look for the cat. He saw the cat from a distance when he went to the top of the barn for hay. It watched him furtively from a safe distance, studying his every movement. We decided to feed the cat twice a day and try to win its trust. It wasn't long before Grandpa named the stray cat Barney.

Each day, Grandpa became more familiar to Barney. He always put a little dish of dry cat food on the barn floor. Sometimes I went up there to give him a special treat of soft cat food, which he so loved. After several weeks, Barney became more curious and friendly. He started coming to eat his food close to Grandpa, who sat quietly on a hay bale. Barney would first call out with a meow, then brush himself against a bale and finally sit nearby, purring for attention.

Barney wouldn't venture too close, until one day Grandpa challenged him to eat from his gloved hand. Barney came within striking distance and sank his claws into the glove, piercing Grandpa's hand.

"Ouch!" Grandpa exclaimed.

Barney had sent out a clear warning: "Look out! I am wild!"

Over time, with much patience and gentleness, Grandpa was able to persuade Barney to sit on his lap while eating. Grandpa was always careful to wear his very thick gloves in case Barney struck out again. There were even a few times when Barney actually let Grandpa stroke his fur while sitting on his lap. I think Grandpa was really brave to trust Barney. Don't you?

Often Barney would situate himself on a little spot jutting out from the barn, giving him a clear view of all the animals eating their hay and Grandpa doing the farm chores below. Barney was a striking cat with orange and white markings of a calico pattern. His face was mostly white, topped with tiny ears and centred with soft green eyes. Barney wanted to be part of our family, but the dogs kept him hiding most of the time. When he needed a drink, he would race to the chicken coop and hide until he could make it safely to the electric watering trough. Angel knew Barney was in the top of the hay barn, but neither cats ever met at close range. Barney was clever and very watchful to keep his distance from everyone except Grandpa.

At the end of March during the Easter weekend, the first real warm day, Barney stopped coming out from the hay bales for his daily feedings. He was gone! Where had he gone? Would he return?

A week later, Barney still hadn't returned. We didn't worry. We knew Barney was a clever cat and quite capable of surviving in the wild. The mild spring temperatures had arrived, with plenty of mice, birds, and other critters scurrying around. Perhaps Barney would have stayed if we had given him sardines or other tasty morsels. We will never know. Every now and then, I think of Barney and hope to see him when I'm out and about.

The following winter, I did see a stray cat race into the bush one day that looked just like Barney. I stopped to ask a neighbour about the calico cat, and sure enough, Barney had found another kind family who cared for his needs that winter when he didn't return to our barn. I was so happy for Barney's survival.

Have you ever rescued or taken in a helpless critter or homeless person? God has a lot to say about rescuing the needy and helpless. My prayers were very quickly answered that bitterly cold day. God cares about His creation, and so should we. Perhaps you can start praying that God will give you opportunities to show His mercy and love to someone who needs your help.

Be encouraged to reach out and help others by the following verses:

> He raises the poor from the dust and lifts the needy from the ash heap, to make them sit with princes, with the princes of his people. He gives the barren woman a home, making her the joyous mother of children. Praise the Lord!
>
> (Psalm 113:7-9)

> ...blessed is he who is generous to the poor.
>
> (Proverbs 14:21)

Devotional Twenty-Six:
Pet Goats

GOATS ARE SO MUCH FUN, BUT WATCH OUT FOR THEIR mischievous behaviour! Our family had pet goats for several years. Our first three goats were males with long horns. We quickly learned that goats need high fences, lots of supervision, and special attention. Goats are curious and playful, forever seeking out trouble. Chewing hair and nibbling on clothing is a common antic and they really enjoy jumping up or butting children smaller than them. They are fussy eaters and will not eat food that falls to the ground, or grass that's too short. Our goats were expert escape artists, often invading the nearest flower or vegetable garden for a gourmet meal. Goats have a way of communicating when they're hungry or lonely. They will baa or cry until someone comes running to answer their pleas. Definitely, goats are nags that "get your goat" if you're a softy.

Goats will bond with other creatures, especially horses that live alone. We had a horse named Cheyenne who patiently enjoyed the company of two kid goats. He bonded to one goat who would often chew his tail, stand on his back when lying down in the pasture, and share his hay and small stall when it was raining. Peace and harmony naturally flowed between Cheyenne and the friendly kid goats.

Goats have a way of getting into your heart, unless of course you're a little tyke and happen to get butted or knocked over. Our grandchildren were often intimidated by our goats. One day, I also happened to get intimidated by a strong milking doe named Maemae. She had a very independent nature. My daughter Grace and I took turns milking Maemae. Sometimes Grace would come storming in the house, crying and mad, because Maemae had outwitted her again by kicking the milk bucket over or drinking the milk when Grace wasn't looking.

We had a special milking routine which started with milking Maemae in the milking stand while she ate grain. We then let her out on the pasture with the other goats. One day, it was my turn to milk Maemae before going to work. I was in a rush, so I wore my work clothes. I took her by the collar and opened the gate to lead her to the milking stand in the other stall. Maemae saw her opportunity to escape! She barged through the gate ahead of me. I had a firm grip on her collar, but she was now pulling me off-balance. My hand didn't come loose from her collar. Instead, I fell facedown to the ground. With a groan, I was dragged while trying to release my grip.

She didn't wait for me to let go. There was a sharp pain in my shoulder, but I tried to ignore the pain and instead focus on securing Maemae before she could take off into the pasture. Too late! She was gone, and there was no catching her. It took me a moment to get up. Maemae dragged me through the mud, leaving me with a wounded ego and a very dirty outfit. Needless to say, I didn't try to catch a stubborn goat that refused to be milked.

I headed for the house to make a quick change. She would have to suffer a full udder until the evening milking. Later that day, my shoulder began to ache, and by the next day I knew my injury was serious. Maemae had torn a tendon in my shoulder. It took over five months to heal after considerable pain and limitation of use.

I never blamed Maemae for my injury or pain. There were many lessons to learn from one stubborn and strong-willed goat. All of life's failures and mishaps are opportunities to learn and grow. I often chuckle now when I think of Maemae. How could a goat be so difficult?

Eventually, Grace and I decided to sell of our goats to another farmer who had much more milking experience and a better setup. We bought our milk from them and often visited our strong-willed Maemae. Cheyenne was short-changed in losing two friends, but his tail did grow longer to help keep the flies away that summer.

Do you have someone or something in your life that's really trying to "get your goat"? Someone or something that's pulling you in the wrong direction, getting you frustrated and upset, like Maemae? If your answer is yes, then you have a challenge not to become angry, frustrated, or mean. Pray and ask God for help. God wants you to be wise and not let life knock you down. Trust

God for an answer to your problem and then obey Him. Let God heal your hurts and pains and get back up to keep experiencing life to the fullest. Let the Lord take revenge and do not pay back evil for evil.

> Repay no one evil for evil, but give thought to do what is honorable in the sight of all. If possible, so far as it depends on you, live peaceably with all. Beloved, never avenge yourselves, but leave it to the wrath of God, for it is written, "Vengeance is mine, I will repay, says the Lord."
>
> (Romans 12:17-19)

> The steps of a man are established by the Lord, when he delights in his way; though he fall, he shall not be cast headlong, for the Lord upholds his hand.
>
> (Psalm 37:23-24)

Devotional Twenty-Seven:
Cariboo Winter

WHEN WINTER COMES, EVERYONE MUST BE PREPARED! Some days can be −30°C, with the wind making it closer to −38°C. Grandpa and I had to experience this cold temperature many times a day when we fed all three horses morning, noon, afternoon, and evening. Every morning we woke up to a cold silence, with the sun just beginning to rise at 8:00 a.m. Grandpa and I reluctantly rolled out of our snug, warm bed, greeted by a cold floor and frosty windows. Chores had to come first before breakfast. I already got up much earlier to add wood to the stove or we would wake up to an ice-cold house.

This was no ordinary chore day, because we couldn't go out unless we put on extra clothing, such as ski pants, ear muffs, ski jacket, two layers of gloves, wool socks, and forty-below boots. There was only six inches of snow on the ground, which you could easily kick away like sugary powder. The trees weren't happy, and neither were the horses. My nose hairs stood on end and stiffened as I breathed in the cold air. Our horses, Rocky and Prince, had icicles from their muzzles. They stood on stilettos, teetering back and forth with snow-clod feet. Rocky's ears pressed down hard and his head swung back in annoyance of the cold. Prince was more of a trooper and just hung his head, waiting for food and more food and more food. Their furry bodies had a light dusting of snow interspersed with clinging icicles. The ground showed where one of them had done a roll in the snow, probably making snow angels.

We did the chores as quickly as possible. Water buckets had to be filled carefully so as not to spill water down the edges of the hose, where a skating rink would eventually form. We skillfully balanced several water buckets back and forth so water wouldn't drizzle down our boots. Some days, we had a fresh foot of new snow, so all the paths to the barn and around the house had to be made all over again.

The most difficult job was removing the many piles of frozen manure in front of the barn where the horses ate their night hay. First, the piles were hit hard with a sharp shovel until they flew into the air like a flat pancake ready to flip. Then all the chunks were gathered into the wheelbarrow that had to be pushed through the trodden snow to dump on a gigantic manure pile. Care was taken not to touch anything metal with wet hands, or our skin would stick like contact cement. My eyelashes froze together if I stayed out too long and my breath became steamy under my face-guard. Everything looked like a dream world. The snow sparkled and danced like diamonds in the air and on every bough and snowdrift.

Once the farm chores were finished, we escaped the cold for a hearty breakfast of the usual huge bowl of steaming porridge with hidden melted blueberries, bananas, raisins, cinnamon, maple syrup, and goat's milk. Mmm! Grandpa did some indoor chores and went downstairs to relax and hope that the sun would come out and warm up the day.

After lunch, we braved the outdoors again with our dogs, Lady and Annie. Lady, in her layers of blubber and fur, kept very warm, and Annie, in her plaid sheepskin coat, was somewhat warm. We all headed for the trails beside our property. Our journey led us to follow numerous animal tracks amongst the trees, seeing where they might lead. We eventually ended up on the wide trail heading home. Lady was unusually slow. When I took a closer look, I noticed big beads of snow and ice under her paws. She would stop and try to bite them off, but to no avail. I urged her along until we got home and put her in the house to melt big puddles on the floor.

Grandpa and I walked down the road to visit our neighbours, Neil and Georgia. Our timing wasn't good, as they were busy when we got there, so off we trudged home. That was when we realized our big mistake! The wind had been at our backs on the way there, but it was on our faces for the return journey. We didn't have face protection, so I held up my gloves as a shield. I had to stop and laugh at Grandpa's face: it was all red and his moustache had turned pure frosty white. He also had a faucet under his nose. Winter in the Cariboo really makes people look funny and teaches you to respect the outdoors.

We noticed that there were no birds that day. Henry, our next door neighbour, thought they might be hiding in the forest. Feeling sorry for the poor critters, we left a big hunk of bread out for them to feast on. There were many animal tracks in the snow going in all directions, but no life to be seen or heard. The snow was so noisy when the horses moved around that it went *squeak-squeak*, not *crunch-crunch*, as I thought it would. Grandpa and I had to learn how to keep warm on those cold days and help the horses to keep warm, too! Grandpa put up a red heat lamp in the barn for the horses to eat under. Grandpa's horse, Vinny, did well, because he had lived through many Cariboo winters, making his fur thick and hardy.

Everyone who lives in our part of the Cariboo loves the snowy cold winters. For at least five months, the fir and pine trees are draped in snow and the frozen ground is blanketed several feet deep. The numerous lakes freeze over, making a winter wonderland of pure white for miles. Winter is a paradise for snow adventures such as cross-country skiing, snow-shoeing, ice-fishing, snowmobiling, and sledding.

The Cariboo winters of endless pure white snow remind me of the real paradise that awaits us in heaven, where everything is pure, bright, and new. Heaven is a real place, even though we cannot see it now. Jesus said,

> Let not your hearts be troubled. Believe in God; believe also in me. In my Father's house are many rooms. If it were not so, would I have told you that I go to prepare a place for you? And if I go and prepare a place for you, I will come again and will take you to myself, that where I am you may be also. And you know the way to where I am going.

(John 14:1–4)

Jesus is speaking of his home in heaven.

Recently, our family and friends were greatly encouraged by a special true story from a young boy. At bedtime one night, his father was talking with him about praying in the name of Jesus whenever he was afraid. The boy shared with his dad an experience he'd had one night. He had awoken from a nightmare and was terribly afraid. As he began to pray in Jesus' name, he suddenly found that he was walking hand in hand with Jesus in heaven. The first person he met was his grandmother, who had recently passed away. Overjoyed to see him, she gave him a big hug. Then Jesus walked with him across bridges and over rivers. Amazing colours were all around! He saw a little boy who was wearing a blue robe, and he knew who this boy was. The little boy had been at church a few years earlier as a little baby, and he had died from a rare disease. The little boy didn't look sick anymore. He was totally healed!

This little boy was our grandson, Owen, who had died at the age of seven months old. Was this a dream or a vision that this young boy shared with his dad? We don't know the answer, but we do know that this boy had an experience in heaven with Jesus, and we do know that Owen is now perfectly whole and happy with Jesus. Heaven is real! All of this life on earth, no matter how beautiful, cannot compare to what God has prepared for those who have Jesus in their heart.

About the Author

My life ministry over the past thirty-four years has focused on children and young adults. I earned my Professional Teaching Certificate from U.B.C. and took two years of training from Child Evangelism International. I also took two years of Bible school. I have experience as a Sunday school teacher, Sunday school superintendent, youth group leader, Vacation Bible School director, child evangelism leader, and director of creation evangelism for youth. My role at home included homeschooling and hospitality to many children and young people. My favorite hobby is writing curriculum for Christian education and writing stories. At present, I am director and teacher of Dream Canada International (née GLEEM Canada), a successful foreign youth discipleship training ministry from 2001 to 2014.